GLOBALVIEWPOINTS

Religious Clothing in Public Spaces

Other Books in the Global Viewpoints Series

GLOBALVIEWPOINTS

Religious Clothing in Public Spaces

Pete Schauer, Book Editor

GREENHAVEN PUBLISHING

Published in 2019 by Greenhaven Publishing, LLC
353 3rd Avenue, Suite 255, New York, NY 10010

Cover image: Gideon Mendel/Corbis via Getty Images

Library of Congress Cataloging-in-Publication Data

Names: Schauer, Pete, editor.
Title: Religious clothing in public spaces / Pete Schauer, book editor.
Description: First Edition. | New York : Greenhaven Publishing, 2018. |
  Series: Global viewpoints | Includes bibliographical references and index. | Audience:
  Grades 9–12.
Identifiers: LCCN 2018005370| ISBN 9781534503526 (library bound) | ISBN
  9781534503533 (pbk.)
Subjects: LCSH: Clothing and dress—Religious aspects.
Classification: LCC BL65.C64 R45 2018 | DDC 323.44/2—dc23
LC record available at https://lccn.loc.gov/2018005370

Manufactured in the United States of America

Website: http://greenhavenpublishing.com

Contents

The hijab is part of Muslim women's religious faith, but it has also been a social obstacle to making friends and developing relationships for some.

Chapter 2: Women and Religious Clothing in Public Spaces

Chapter 3: Religious Clothing and Public Schools

Chapter 4: Dealing with Religious Clothing in Public Spaces

Foreword

> *"The problems of all of humanity can
> only be solved by all of humanity."*
> *—Swiss author Friedrich Dürrenmatt*

Global interdependence has become an undeniable reality. Mass media and technology have increased worldwide access to information and created a society of global citizens. Understanding and navigating this global community is a challenge, requiring a high degree of information literacy and a new level of learning sophistication.

Building on the success of its flagship series, Opposing Viewpoints, Greenhaven Publishing has created the Global Viewpoints series to examine a broad range of current, often controversial topics of worldwide importance from a variety of international perspectives. Providing students and other readers with the information they need to explore global connections and think critically about worldwide implications, each Global Viewpoints volume offers a panoramic view of a topic of widespread significance.

Drugs, famine, immigration— a broad, international treatment is essential to do justice to social, environmental, health, and political issues such as these. Junior high, high school, and early college students, as well as general readers, can all use Global Viewpoints anthologies to discern the complexities relating to each issue. Readers will be able to examine unique national perspectives while, at the same time, appreciating the interconnectedness that global priorities bring to all nations and cultures.

Material in each volume is selected from a diverse range of sources, including journals, magazines, newspapers, nonfiction books, speeches, government documents, pamphlets, organization newsletters, and position papers. Global Viewpoints is truly global, with material drawn primarily from international sources available in English and secondarily from US sources with extensive international coverage.

Features of each volume in the Global Viewpoints series include:

- An **annotated table of contents** that provides a brief summary of each essay in the volume, including the name of the country or area covered in the essay.

- An **introduction** specific to the volume topic.

- A **world map** to help readers locate the countries or areas covered in the essays.

- For each viewpoint, an **introduction** that contains notes about the author and source of the viewpoint explains why material from the specific country is being presented, summarizes the main points of the viewpoint, and offers three **guided reading questions** to aid in understanding and comprehension.

- **For further discussion questions** that promote critical thinking by asking the reader to compare and contrast aspects of the viewpoints or draw conclusions about perspectives and arguments.

- A worldwide list of **organizations to contact** for readers seeking additional information.

- A **periodical bibliography** for each chapter and a **bibliography of books** on the volume topic to aid in further research.

- A comprehensive **subject index** to offer access to people, places, events, and subjects cited in the text.

Global Viewpoints is designed for a broad spectrum of readers who want to learn more about current events, history, political science, government, international relations, economics, environmental science, world cultures, and sociology—students doing research for class assignments or debates, teachers and faculty seeking to supplement course materials, and others wanting to understand current issues better. By presenting how people in various countries perceive the root causes, current consequences, and proposed solutions to worldwide challenges, Global Viewpoints volumes offer readers opportunities to enhance their global awareness and their knowledge of cultures worldwide.

Introduction

> *"After a decade of legal uncertainty over the wearing of the headscarf in state schools, the French government in 2004 banned all 'conspicuous' religious symbols, including the Muslim headscarf, from public institutions such as state schools or town halls. This was followed in 2010 by what the French call the 'burqa ban,' outlawing the full face covering in public."*
> —The Economist, July 7, 2014.

For many people around the world, religion is not just a set of beliefs, but rather a way of life. Religion comes in all different types of forms, values, and faith, and it is what helps give people their identity. But when that identity is stripped away, it can lead to controversy and unrest in one's country. Wearing religious clothing and attire in public spaces has become an issue of debate in various countries around the world, even leading to the banning of religious attire in some public areas. The ban has primarily revolved around full-face veils, also known as burqas and niqabs that are worn by Muslim women. Sometimes also known as headscarves, these articles of religious clothing cover the heads, necks, and sometimes faces of women of the Muslim religion, serving as a sign of religious faith.

Led by France, many European countries have enforced the ban on full-face veils, and this has resulted in the questioning of secularism, or the separation between the state and the religion.

The separation of religion and state is the foundation of secularism, but if the state is intervening and banning the wearing of certain religious articles of clothing in public, they are interfering in religious affairs and breaking the foundation of secularism.

The French ban on full-face coverings was established in 2011 and has since divided the nation. Those who are in favor of the ban believe that the wearing of full-face coverings prevents the ability to identify who a person is—which is a security risk—and that forcing women to wear this kind of religious garb is sexist. Those who are against the ban believe that it intrudes on individual and religious freedom, discriminates against the Muslim culture, and affects women's rights to make decisions for themselves.

On that note, women's rights is a common theme that runs through this issue. On one hand, making it mandatory that women wear a certain article of clothing can be seen, particularly by westerners, as controlling and demeaning, but on the other hand, banning these articles of clothing and denying women of the right to express their religious beliefs is also stripping women of their rights.

Another branch of the debate is the prohibiting of wearing religious articles of clothing in public schools, and that goes for both students and teachers. While it varies country to country, in the United States, teachers have a lot more restrictions on religious expression within the school than the students do. For example, public school teachers are only able to teach religion if it is objective, teaching students about the role of religion throughout the course of history. They are prohibited from sharing their personal religious beliefs or trying to steer students in a certain religious direction. Students, on the other hand, are permitted to pray individually or discuss their religion with other students as long as it is done in a respectful, non-disruptive manner. Students are also allowed to wear religious clothing as long as it is not offensive. The laws are much different in France, however, where the French law bans the wearing of any religious symbols or clothing in French public schools.

The viewpoints in *Global Viewopints: Religious Clothing in Public Spaces* explore this difficult issue through enlightening perspectives from around the world. Readers will hear from people on many sides of the issue, from government officials who ruled in favor of the ban to Muslim women who feel oppressed and speak out against the banning of their religious garb. The thoughtful examinations of the complex debate may change some readers' minds about where they stand on the issue.

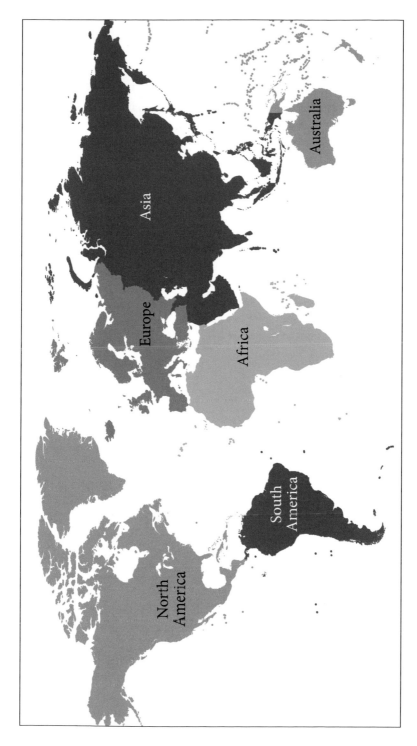

GLOBALVIEWPOINTS

CHAPTER 1

Religious Clothing in Public Spaces Around the World

In Catalonia a Burqa Ban Leads to Serious Threats

Soeren Kern

In the following viewpoint, Soeren Kern reports on terrorist threats by a jihadist group that is affiliated with Al Qaeda in Catalonia, a region in northeastern Spain. The terrorist group, called Africamuslima, made the threats in response to Catalonian lawmakers increasing surveillance of radical Salafists who were looking to enforce Islamic Sharia law in Spain in addition to the Catalan Parliament taking strides toward banning Muslim burqas and niqabs in all public spaces. It is important to note that the lawmakers were also looking to prohibit the wearing of all forms of face coverings, meaning items such as motorcycle helmets and masks would also be banned in public. Kern is is a Senior Fellow at the Gatestone Institute and Senior Fellow for European Politics at the Grupo de Estudios Estratégicos/ Strategic Studies Group.

As you read, consider the following questions:

1. How many people live in Catalonia?
2. How many Muslims are estimated to live in Catalonia?
3. What is Salafism?

"Spain: Jihadists Threaten Catalonia over Burqa Ban," by Soeren Kern, Originally published by Gatestone Institute, September 13, 2013. Reprinted by permission.

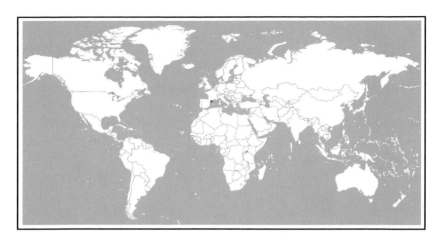

A jihadist group affiliated with Al Qaeda has threatened to carry out terrorist attacks in Catalonia, an autonomous region in northeastern Spain that is home to the largest concentration of radical Islamists in Europe.

The threats were issued by a group called "Africamuslima" in response to efforts by Catalonian lawmakers to increase surveillance of radical Salafists seeking to impose Islamic Sharia law in Spain and other parts of Europe.

Catalonia—a region of 7.5 million people centered on the Mediterranean city of Barcelona—is home to the largest Muslim population in Spain. Most of the estimated 450,000 Muslims in Catalonia are from the Middle East, North Africa and South Asia.

Many of the Muslims living in Catalonia are shiftless single males who are unemployed and "susceptible to jihadist recruitment," according to diplomatic cables obtained by Wikileaks and published by the Madrid-based *El País* newspaper.

Spanish authorities are especially concerned about the threat posed by Salafism, a radical strain of Islam that seeks to re-establish an Islamic empire [Caliphate] across the Middle East, North Africa and Spain, which Salafists view as a Muslim state that must be reconquered for Islam.

Spain's National Intelligence Center [CNI] says Catalonia is home to hundreds and possibly thousands of Salafists who, according to intelligence experts, pose the greatest threat to Spain's national security.

Catalan officials recently have redoubled efforts to improve surveillance of Salafist groups in the region.

On August 27, it emerged that Catalan police (known locally as the Mossos d'Esquadra) have been conducting a "census" to identify and register Muslim women who wear Islamic body-covering burqas and face-covering niqabs.

According to local media reports, the Catalan Interior Minister, Ramon Espadaler—based on the belief that these garments may constitute an indicator of the spread of Salafism in Catalonia—has ordered members of the Mossos to file a report every time they see a burqa or niqab.

Espadaler said the effort involves creating a "list of indicators that could point us to radicalization processes." He warned that there is a "target risk" of radicalization in Muslim areas in Catalonia, and made it clear that the collection of data on burqas and niqabs is part of the requirement that the Mossos "remain vigilant."

Catalan government spokesman Francesc Homs defended the move; he said that police have an obligation to "know what is going on."

On July 18, the Catalan Parliament approved a draft law that would ban the wearing of face-coverings such as the Muslim burqa or niqab in all public spaces. The proposed ban is set to become an integral part of a new Law on Pubic Spaces that will be presented to the Parliament in early 2014.

In an effort to avoid being accused of singling out Muslims, the Catalan Interior Ministry has sought to frame the proposed burqa ban within the context of public safety. As a result, it has extended the proposed ban to prohibit the wearing of all forms of face coverings, including masks and motorcycle helmets, within public buildings.

In February 2013, the Spanish Supreme Court ruled that a municipal ordinance banning the wearing of Islamic burqas in public spaces was unconstitutional.

In its 56-page ruling, the Madrid-based Tribunal Supremo said the Catalan city of Lérida exceeded its authority when it imposed a burqa ban in December 2010.

The court further said the ban on burqas "constitutes a limitation to the fundamental right to the exercise of the freedom of religion, which is guaranteed by the Spanish constitution." The court added that the limitation of a fundamental right can only be achieved through laws at the national level, not through local ordinances.

The decision, which the court said addressed a "profoundly political problem," represented a significant victory for Muslims in Spain. Although it is unclear how many women actually wear the burqa there, the ruling denoted a step forward in the continuing efforts to establish Islam as a mainstream religious and political system in Spain.

It remains to be seen whether Catalonia will succeed in its effort to circumvent the Supreme Court ruling by reframing the debate over burqas as an issue of public safety rather than one of freedom of religion.

The proposed burqa ban has already drawn the ire of Salafi jihadists, who are determined to quash any resistance to the rise of Islam in Spain.

In a three-page document dated August 28, Africamuslima—a little-known jihadist group with links to Al Qaeda in the Islamic Maghreb—rebukes "the Nazi gestures of the Catalan government" and warns that moves to "scapegoat Muslims for Catalonia's institutional and economic failures" by regulating the burqa "will not remain without a response."

"We note the history of hatred and mistreatment of the Muslim community in Catalonia on the part of the government and its goons [Mossos]," the document states. "We have been following the situation in hopes that things would change. However, the only thing we have observed is an increase in the mistreatment of the Muslim community that is without equal in all of Europe."

The document posits a series of rhetorical questions: "Democracy? And they [the Catalan authorities] want to interfere in the way in which women dress? What will be next? The establishment of concentration camps for Muslims who refuse to wear the types of clothing dictated by the Catalan government?"

Africamuslima then lists five specific complaints, including the "denial of permits for the construction of mosques," "the indiscriminate detention of Muslims," "the institutional and financial support for organizations promoting a Nazi ideology with the clear objective to intimidate the Muslim community," "the exclusion of [unemployed] Muslims from the public health and social welfare system," and "the exclusion of Muslim children from meal voucher benefits [in public schools]."

Some of these complaints refer to economic austerity measures in Catalonia that have dramatically restricted the availability of social welfare benefits—including free meal vouchers in public schools—to Spanish families across the board, regardless of race or religion.

The document concludes by urging Catalan media, as well as Catalan political and cultural elites, to "distance themselves from the incendiary, racist and xenophobic discourse" that is promoting "fear of the other."

Africamuslima warns that "blaming Muslims will not solve your [economic] problems but will bring you misfortune." It adds that "any action taken against Muslim women will be met with a response against Catalan interests both inside of and outside of Catalonia."

The text is signed by an individual calling himself Karim Al-Maghribi, who, because of his knowledge of the social issues of the region, Spanish intelligence analysts believe may be living inside Catalonia.

Ramon Espadaler, the Catalan Interior Minister, says the proposed burqa ban has nothing to do with "religious issues. It is not a general prohibition. That would lead us nowhere and we would be infringing on fundamental rights." He added: "We want to be sensitive…we want a careful, subtle and clear debate to find a consensus."

In Spain the Growing Muslim Population Is Resulting in a Burqa Ban

Soeren Kern

In the following viewpoint, Soeren Kern discusses the potential for a ban on burqas and niqabs in all public places across Spain. This is an issue on many levels, especially considering the fact that nearly 70 percent of Spanish Muslims identify themselves as primarily Muslim instead of Spanish. Kern also writes that Muslims feel that the territories they lost during the Spanish Reconquest still belong to them, due to the Islamic idea that Muslim territories must remain under Muslim domination forever. It is important to note that the ban would not include mantilla shawls, or head-covering veils, which are worn by Spanish women. Kern is is a Senior Fellow at the Gatestone Institute and Senior Fellow for European Politics at the Grupo de Estudios Estratégicos/Strategic Studies Group.

As you read, consider the following questions:

1. For about how many years did Muslims rule large parts of Spain?
2. Nearly what percentage of Spanish Muslims identify themselves as primarily Muslim?
3. What percentage of Spain's population do Muslims make up?

"Spain Debates Burqa Ban; Muslim Immigration Soars," by Soeren Kern, Originally published by Gatestone Institute., July 21, 2010. Reprinted by permission.

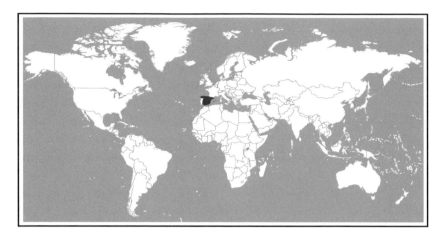

The lower house of the Spanish Parliament is debating a proposal to prohibit the wearing of body-covering burqas and face-covering niqabs in all public spaces in Spain. The measure, which follows similar moves by nearly a dozen local and regional governments across Spain, marks a major escalation in the national debate over Muslim immigration and the role of radical Islam in Spain.

Critics say the rate of Muslim immigration to Spain now far exceeds the rate of assimilation. And polls seem to support that claim. According to a Pew Global Attitudes Survey, for example, religion is central to the identity of Spanish Muslims. Nearly 70 percent of Spanish Muslims identify themselves primarily as Muslim rather than as Spanish. This level of Muslim identification in Spain is similar to that in Pakistan, Nigeria, and Jordan, and even higher than levels in Egypt, Turkey, and Indonesia.

There is now a widespread feeling among Muslims that the territories they lost during the Spanish Reconquest still belong to them, and that they have a right to return and establish their rule there. This is based on the Islamic idea that territories once occupied by Muslims must remain under Muslim domination forever.

The majority of Muslim immigrants to Spain are from Morocco, Algeria and Pakistan. They mostly live in clusters along the Mediterranean coast. Fully one-third of Spain's Muslims live in the north-eastern autonomous region of Catalonia, the capital of which is Barcelona. Tarragona, one of the most important cities in Catalonia, has also become ground-zero for Salafist Islam in Spain.

Salafism is a branch of revivalist Islam that calls for restoring past Muslim glory by re-establishing an Islamic empire across the Middle East, North Africa and parts of Europe. Salafists view Spain as a Muslim state that must be reconquered for Islam.

Muslims ruled large parts of Spain for a period of about 800 years. Islamic rule over the region then known as Al-Andalus ended in 1492, when Granada, the last Muslim stronghold, capitulated to the Roman Catholic kings.

In Granada, for example, there are now parallel societies and some Muslims want traditional Sharia law to be applied there instead of Spanish law. They are also demanding Muslim education and special Muslim schools for their children. They even want an equal share in the money made with ticket sales for the fabled Alhambra palace, which they regard as part of the cultural heritage of their Muslim ancestors.

The debate comes after the Spanish Senate, on June 23, voted 131 to 129 to "use all options under our legal system and to proceed with rules to prohibit the public use of the 'burqa' and the 'niqab' to ensure equality, freedom and security." The Senate language also calls on Spain to outlaw "any usage, custom or discriminatory practice that limits the freedom of women."

Leaders of the ruling Socialist Party have said they support the proposal, which was introduced by the opposition center-right Popular Party. Spanish Justice Minister Francisco Caamaño said that full-face veils such as the burqa are "hardly compatible with human dignity." The unusual display of bipartisan unity on the burqa issue makes a ban likely unless Spain's highest court rules it unconstitutional. A final vote on the ban is expected to take place in early September, after the summer holidays.

The burqa debate comes as immigration from Muslim countries to Spain continues to soar. Spain currently has a Muslim population of slightly over 1 million, or about 2 percent of Spain's total population. Although this percentage is smaller than in other European countries such as France (7 percent), Holland (6 percent), Belgium (4 percent), Germany (3 percent) and Britain (3 percent), Spain has experienced a whopping ten-fold increase in the number of Muslim immigrants in just 20 years.

As recently as 1990, there were only 100,000 Muslims in Spain. Up until the 1980s, Spain was a net exporter of labor and there was very little Muslim labor immigration to the country. Instead, Spain was a transit country for Maghrebian [North African} immigrants on their way to France and other European countries with significant and well-established Muslim communities. But during the mid-1990s, Spain's traditional role as a transit country became that of a host country for Muslim immigrants, especially from Morocco.

Immigration, however, is only one reason for the steady rise in Spain's Muslim population. Muslim fertility rates are more than double those of an aging native Spanish population. Spain currently has a birth rate of around 1.3, which is far below the replacement rate of 2.1 children per couple. At the current rates, the number of native Spaniards will be cut in half in two generations, while the Muslim population in Spain will quadruple.

Another survey sponsored by the Spanish government shows that only 46 percent of Muslim immigrants can understand, speak and read in Spanish without problems.

The Pew survey also shows that Muslim immigrants are viewed with suspicion by Spanish society and that most Spaniards doubt that Muslims coming to Spain want to adopt their national customs and way of life. Almost 70 percent of Spaniards say that Muslims in Spain want to remain distinct from the larger society.

Almost 80 percent of the Spanish public sees Muslims as having a strong Islamic identity. Among those in the Spanish general public who see Islamic identity on the rise, 82 percent say it is a bad thing. Around 65 percent of Spaniards are somewhat or very concerned about rising Islamic extremism in their country.

In October 2007, Amr Moussa, the Egyptian Secretary-General of the Arab League, asked the Spanish government to allow Muslims to worship in the cathedral of Córdoba. This building was a mosque during the medieval Islamic kingdom of Al-Andalus. Muslims now hope to recreate the ancient city of Córdoba, which was once the heart of Al-Andalus, as a pilgrimage site for Muslims throughout Europe. Funds for the project are being sought from the governments of the United Arab Emirates and Kuwait, and Muslim organizations in Morocco and Egypt.

The debate over Muslim immigration and radical Islam in Spain recently flared when an imam in Tarragona was arrested for forcing a woman to wear a hijab head covering. The local prosecutor had asked the judge to jail the imam and three others for five years for harassment, but the case was eventually dismissed after the Socialist mayor said she wanted to prevent "a social conflict."

In another case, nine Salafists in Catalonia kidnapped a woman, tried her for adultery based on Sharia law, and condemned her to death. The woman escaped and fled to a local police station just before she was to be executed by the Islamists.

Not surprisingly, the Spanish debate over banning the burqa is especially heated in Catalonia, where nearly a dozen municipalities have banned the use of Islamic veils in public. In June, Barcelona was the first major Spanish city to bar the use of face-covering Islamic veils in municipal buildings.

In the Catalan town of Lleida, where 29,000 Muslims make up more than 20 percent of the town's population, the town council recently voted to ban the burqa in all public spaces. Women found wearing burqas will be let off with a warning, but second offenders will be fined up to €600 ($750).

The burqa issue burst onto the national stage last November, when a Muslim lawyer was ejected from Spain's high court in Madrid, where she was defending a client, because the lawyer refused to remove her headscarf. And in April, a 16-year-old schoolgirl was banned from a school in Madrid after refusing to remove her hijab, in violation of the school dress code. That decision sparked a debate because there are no clear guidelines over the wearing of Islamic headdresses in state schools in Spain.

The proposed burqa ban, which has the support of all of Spain's major political parties except for those on the extreme left, would not include head-covering veils, such as the mantilla shawls often worn by Spanish women, especially during religious ceremonies in southern Spain.

If the burqa ban is approved by the Spanish Parliament, it will still need to be vetted by the Supreme Court to determine its compatibility with the Spanish Constitution and the European Convention on Human Rights. The Council of Europe, the European institution dealing with human rights issues, recently warned national governments against imposing a complete ban, saying that it would constitute an "ill-advised invasion of individual privacy."

In the United States Public School Districts Must Run a Fine Line When It Comes to Religion

Center for Public Education

In the following viewpoint, the Center for Public Education discusses the ground rules when it comes to the separation between religion and the US public school system. These ground rules are based off of the First Amendment to the Constitution, which says citizens have the right to freely exercise religious beliefs, but also that public schools are prohibited from establishing religion. As the CPE writes, there is a fine line that teachers and administrators must run so that personal religious beliefs are allowed, but that none are favored more than others or given special treatment. The Center for Public Education is a national resource for information about public education in the United States.

As you read, consider the following questions:

1. What month of the year is likely the most difficult to manage for public schools when it comes to religion?
2. How many words does the Constitution use that are known as the "religion clauses?"
3. The US is home to more than how many religions?

"Religion and Public Schools," Center for Public Education, April 5, 2006. Reprinted by permission.

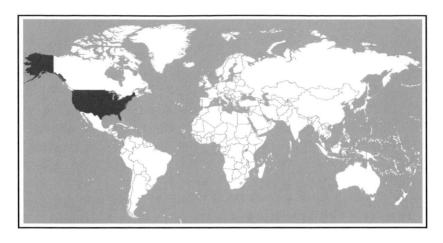

When it comes to religion, public schools must obey two legal requirements that are hard to reconcile: let it be, and push it away. These are the clashing and equally forceful commands contained in the First Amendment to the U.S. Constitution.

The Constitution uses 16 words—known as the "religion clauses"—to create rules about how faith and government interact. One clause gives citizens the right to freely exercise religious convictions; the other prohibits government (including taxpayer-funded public schools) from establishing religion, meaning granting favorable treatment.

Yet, because the Constitution is so brief about what's expected and so vague on how to do it, the result has been years of conflict and strife. The main questions:

- How far can students or school staff go in expressing their beliefs?

- When have school officials gone too far in letting religion reign?

What it really amounts to is being fair. Unlike private schools, public school districts are bound by the Constitution, which forces them into a delicate balance. Board members and school administrators are required to allow personal acts of religious faith but to simultaneously avoid any appearance that religion (or any particular religion) enjoys special status. The U.S. Supreme Court has the final word in resolving disputes about what the Constitution permits or forbids.

Among the issues that have reached the High Court:

- Can a school district allow students to conduct prayers over the loudspeaker and before kickoff at a varsity football game? (No)

- Does a religious student club get the same rights and privileges as other student clubs? (Yes)

- Is a school district required to give equal access to an outside organizations that provide after-school religious instruction to young children? (Yes)

- Is a moment of silence really a cloaking device for prayer? (Sometimes)

- Are the words "under God" in the pledge of allegiance unconstitutional in schools? (Undecided)

The duty to uphold the Constitution is a fundamental difference between public schools and religious schools. While government-sponsored schools must stay neutral (often called separation of church and state), private schools are not similarly bound. The contrast is stark: parochial and religious schools openly inculcate religion while teaching reading, writing, and mathematics.

Increasingly, public school leaders describe being seized by a powerful vise grip. On one side: local and national religious organizations that push, then sue if they believe religion is being denied. On the other: civil liberties groups, equally aggressive and equally willing to use federal courts to thwart coziness between religion and school practices.

These types of cases have been around for decades, but as the United States has become increasingly polarized along religious lines, disputes and subsequent lawsuits over religion in the schools have drawn widespread attention on a local, state, and national level.

The following examples show what that tightrope looks like on a day-to-day basis.

- OK: Teaching about the Bible, the Torah, or other sacred texts and their influence on human behavior. No one denies that religion has strongly motivated behavior in the United States and around the world. Acknowledging that fact in the curriculum does not raise First Amendment concerns.

- Wrong: Teaching sacred documents with devotion or as singular truth. It crosses the line when a teacher or school district portrays one religion or religion in general as the preferred belief.

- OK: Allowing a student to wear a T-shirt, wrist band, or neckwear expressing religious belief. As long as the item is not vulgar, insulting, or otherwise inappropriate, school officials cannot interfere with that kind of personal statement.

- Wrong: Forbidding such items or giving special treatment to believers. Problems arise when, for example, a teacher gives higher grades to students who mention "God" in their homework assignment, or district policy prohibits a skull cap (worn by Jewish boys) or Hijab (headscarf worn by Muslim girls) because of their religious connection. The toughest calls under the Constitution come when courts have to balance religious freedom against safety concerns. For example, a student has a right to pray between classes, but can not kneel in the hallway and create a hazard for other students trying to pass. As well, school officials have a keen interest in preventing gang affiliations, but would be hard-pressed to forbid a student from wearing a religious garment that happened to coincide with gang colors.

- OK: Allowing a school-sponsored Gospel Choir that performs praise songs. While the music originates from church, the choir is learning principles of performance, vocal control, and other artistic concepts by participating. The words of faith are viewed as secondary.

- Wrong: Forbidding students or staff to pray between classes or penalizing them for being absent for religious holidays. Contrary to some popular criticism, religion has not been driven out of the schools. As long as a student is not disrupting the normal flow of the school, he or she can say a prayer as desired. Also, in general, students should be allowed time away (briefly during the school day or for a single day or more) to comply with religious tenets.

Generally, conflicts between religion and public schools fall into three categories:

- *Inside Acts*—Arise within school buildings and are based on actions of students or staff (e.g., student religious clubs, clothing and symbols, passing out faith-based literature).

- *Outsider Access*—Includes efforts by external organizations that wish to spread religious messages or use the facility for worship.

- *Curriculum Concerns*—Includes issues such as Intelligent Design, the theory that an "intelligent cause" is the best explanation for the complexity of life (Discovery Institute, 2006), or a full-semester high school course on the Bible.

For non-experts, it can be frustrating to try to make heads or tails of court decisions. Cases can be misleading and seemingly contradictory about what's allowed.

A few things are clear under the Constitution, however. These absolutes are what distinguish public schools from their private or religious K–12 counterparts. The bright lines in the *Establishment and Free Exercise Clauses* strike a peace accord that allows believers and skeptics to peacefully co-exist.

Mormon Underwear

Known to some is the fact that members of The Church of Jesus Christ of Latter-day Saints (or Mormon Church) wear a special kind of underwear in connection with their religion. This is true of most faithful adult members of the Church. (Mormon children are generally dressed the same as any other children.) The special underwear is called a "garment" by Mormons, and it is directly related to Mormon temples.

Garments are a symbolic gesture of the promises that Mormons have made to God. The garment is always worn under other clothing, next to the skin. In fact, for most people who wear it, the garment takes the place of regular underwear. Mormons begin wearing it during their first visit to the temple, wherein they receive individual instruction on how the garment should be worn and cared for, and furthermore, they undergo a sacred ceremony called the temple endowment. Solely during this ritual, additional special clothing is put on; by contrast, the garment or special underwear is worn at all times, both day and night, from then on. It serves as a constant reminder of the covenants made during the temple endowment.

Mormons believe in being "in the world, but not of it," and the garment helps in privately yet consistently setting temple-going Mormons apart from the world. A particularly sharp contrast is felt in today's society, where morals and modesty have deteriorated to a most horrific degree. Many moviemakers and clothing manufacturers, for example, design their respective products to reveal so much of the human body that virtually nothing is left to the imagination. Mormons, on the other hand, are encouraged through the modest length and cut of their temple-got garments to always dress appropriately. Devout Mormons further understand that in only a very few instances might the garment be removed, such as for swimming, using the bathroom, or being intimate in marriage. The reasons for keeping the garment on far outweigh the reasons for taking it off.

"Mormon Underwear," LDSChurchTemples.org.

Establishment Clause

School districts may not endorse (or appear to be endorsing) religious activities in school sponsored activities. What that means in practice is that schools may not give special treatment to believers nor special prominence to activities that highlight religion. The Establishment Clause, in other words, is the Constitutional device that prevents public entities like schools from taking sides with the faith-based community. The need for the divide harkens back to the founding of this country, when the potential for religious strife was a real threat to the unity of a new nation.

A 1971 case called *Lemon v. Kurtzman* remains the leading case on the Establishment Clause and continues to guide the courts in deciding when a school district's action violates the First Amendment. Courts ask a series of three questions in this order:

1. Does it have a secular (non-religious) purpose? That question was key in a 1985 potent "moment of silence or voluntary prayer" case. The U.S. Supreme Court sought to determine whether there was a secular purpose behind a state law passed by the Alabama legislature. Looking at the evidence, justices determined that the morning practice was a back-door way of persuading children to pray, and struck the law down. Therefore, at the outset of a case courts ask: Does the challenged activity have a religious (sectarian) purpose or are there sound secular reasons motivating school officials?

2. Does it advance or inhibit religion? Asking this question gives judges a sense of the neutrality of the practice. Something that advances religion would be a classic Establishment Clause violation. An example would be charging a general fee for a service but exempting religious clubs from the cost. Likewise, inhibiting religion is unconstitutional, and might occur if school districts do the opposite with their fee schedule.

3. Does it cause excessive entanglement with religion? In short, does the government involvement with a religious activity stretch so deep that it is indistinguishable from the religious nature itself. This question seeks to prevent schools and other activities from doing everything they can to support religion and stopping short of saying it out loud. Cooperation with religious causes and accommodation are both permissible, but entanglement occurs when the Constitution puts a halt to the relationship. An example might be an alternative high school where each week the primary speakers at a mandatory assembly are clergy or religious leaders who talk about morality. Entanglement might be an even greater problem if it is only one denomination that is being preferred.

Each question is a hurdle to be crossed. If the answer to the first question is yes, then the case proceeds. The Court's answer to the second and third questions must be no. If the answer is wrong at any stage, then usually an "establishment of religion" is found and the district loses.

The Lemon test remains the standard by which cases are judged. Other theories have been developed by the Supreme Court to make the Lemon test less potent, but it has never been overridden. A case continues forever as prevailing law unless the U.S. Supreme Court outwardly repudiates it and overturns it.

In the 1984 *Lynch v. Donnelly* case, U.S. Supreme Court Justice Sandra Day O'Connor took the first two Lemon questions and said they amount to an "endorsement test." Really, she said, courts should look for whether schools are in effect endorsing religion. That view has been influential. While O'Connor's interpretation does not override Lemon, some courts have adopted her approach in deciding conflicts.

By contrast, U.S. Supreme Court Justice Anthony Kennedy wrote strongly that the better approach was the "coercion test." In *Lee v. Weisman* he wrote that unless government coerces people to support or participate in religion against their will, the religious clauses are not violated. That view, explained in a 1992 case about prayer at graduation ceremonies, would allow for a closer collaboration between government and religion than might otherwise be permitted under O'Connor's idea or the idea that schools must be "neutral."

The Lemon test was revisited in 1997 in a case called *Agostini v. Felton*. The Court said courts should ask whether government indoctrination has occurred, and whether the recipients of government benefit are defined by religion.

The Lemon test, the endorsement test, the coercion test, the Felton question about indoctrination, and the underlying idea of neutrality can all potentially apply when someone challenges a school as violating the Establishment Clause. The fact that there is no single test that can be applied and different theories that could be deployed by the Court depending on the issue is what makes the outcomes unpredictable and causes school officials—and quite candidly school law attorneys—to be confused and occasionally wrong. While that makes for headaches, in some ways the uncertainty is absolutely in line with Constitutional law itself—forcing judges to make decisions by balancing interests on a case-by-case basis rather than on generalizations. Except for the items that are at the margin, it is almost impossible to say on a knee-jerk basis whether an action is or is not an establishment of religion. Decisions by the Supreme Court and federal courts keep moving the line. These days, courts tend to have a broader definition of the Establishment Clause and permit a tighter bind between religion and schools than courts 30 years ago.

Often this question comes into bright contrast in December, with Christmas, Hanukkah, Ramadan, and the non-religious Kwanzaa converging and competing for attention. It is where Establishment and Free Exercise intersect most clearly.

Accusations fly that school officials are establishing religion by plays, music, holiday displays, or discussions in class. Equally fervent accusations fly that school districts are squelching the free exercise of religion by not permitting certain observances in class or during school hours.

Sorting out what's permitted and what's forbidden can be excruciating. And, again, no single Supreme Court decision will lead to the "right" answer. To reach a neutral rendering on holiday displays, the Court has settled into a hodgepodge rule that requires school and other public officials to in some way balance the various religious symbols and to include non-religious symbols.

Free Exercise Clause

- Students can pray in school, if they are not disrupting normal activities.

- Students can be released from class for ritual prayer or leave school early for religious instruction.

- School staff and students can wear religious symbols. Staff items cannot contain proselytizing messages, like "I love Allah and you should too."

- A teacher may not refuse to teach a portion of the approved curriculum on religious grounds.

- The Free Exercise Clause is commonly combined with the First Amendment Free Speech Clause to combat "viewpoint discrimination." Religious speech cannot be treated differently simply because of the subject.

Some summarize the twin Constitutional directives this way: Freedom of religion and Freedom from religion. In recent years that duality has been a magnet for lawsuits. For instance, from 1990 to 2001 the National School Boards Association wrote friend-of-the-court briefs in 21 religion cases heard by the U.S. Supreme Court or federal appeals courts.

Of all the places where Free Exercise applies, the situation that captures public imagination most is the one of prayer. When, where, and how students can pray often becomes a source of conflict. The general rule is that students are free to pursue their faith in school as long as they are not disruptive. Therefore, they can pray silently in class but cannot disrupt a lesson with a spoken prayer. Students can pray during lunch periods or other down time, but cannot skip academic classes to pray. The exception, however, is that some religions require ritual prayer at certain times and in certain ways. Schools have predominantly made provisions for that to happen. There's also a line to be drawn between private individual prayer (often OK) and public group prayer (usually not OK).

So where are the hot spots?

- Religious holidays versus the academic calendar. Controversy flared in Michigan in October 2005, because the state scheduled exams during the Muslim holy days of Ramadan and the Jewish holy days of Rosh Hashannah and Yom Kippur. The incident highlights the growing need for school leaders to be aware of and sensitive to religious observances.

- School-sponsored speech. The key 1992 Supreme Court decision, *Lee v. Weisman,* struck down a school district's practice of inviting clergy to lead prayer at graduation. More recently: In October 2004, a federal appeals court sided with a Florida school district, saying officials were right to remove a student's religious message from the mural she painted for a school beautification project. The case, *Bannon v. School District of Palm Beach County*, was appealed to the U.S. Supreme Court, which in October of 2005, declined to hear it.

- Concerns about subtle religious inculcation. Into this category fall issues such as posting the 10 Commandments and school involvement by the faith-based community. School officials must be mindful that outward acts carry the risk that viewers or listeners could mistakenly believe that the district is officially supporting religious sentiment.

- Student group and outside group access. On the side of student groups is The Equal Access Act, a federal law that applies to secondary schools. Key case: *Board of Education of Westside Community Schools v. Mergens.* Likewise, outside groups will continue to push for opportunities to spread their view. Key case: *Good News Club v. Milford Central School.*

- Expressions of Faith by Staff Members. Faculty advisors of religious clubs and technology issues, such as employees who place religious taglines at the end of e-mail, are just two instances where conflict has occurred. Developments in this area call for school officials to balance the rights of the employee and the special needs of school environment.

- Teaching About Religion. Including a 2005 book, *The Bible and Its Influence*, and curriculum that examines the Bible's affect on literature, art, history, and culture are potential hotbeds of contention. The Fairfax, Virginia-based Bible Literacy Project says about 300 school districts are considering the course. While the idea of teaching and learning about religious subjects is standard, schools must resist the temptation to tilt the curriculum toward a particular religion or otherwise compromise their non-committal stance.

- Class assignments. As long as the religious aspects meet assignment requirements, there is no problem. The challenge: When work will be displayed or the student uses a class speech to preach to a captive audience.

As we look to the future, the battle will surely continue. Scholars say the United States is home to more than 2,000 religions and about 400,000 churches, synagogues, and mosques. The public's schools are a natural battleground, supporting 90 percent of all school-aged children nationwide. Public schools are also where youngsters develop values—particularly at young, impressionable ages.

Equally challenging is the fact that federal and U.S. Supreme Court decisions keep shifting the standards and expectations for public schools—another hurdle that private schools need not clear. The Constitution ensures that every student who receives public schooling has the opportunity to express his or her sincerely held belief, or to be free from the unwelcome pressure to believe at all.

The Headscarf Has Caused a Lot of Controversy

The Pluralism Project at Harvard University

In the following viewpoint, the Pluralism Project at Harvard University discusses the various controversies surrounding the headscarf. The controversial locations include the countries of France and Germany, and even a town in Oklahoma called Muskogee. The Muskogee issue stemmed from an 11-year-old girl being suspended two separate times for wearing a Muslim headscarf to school. Eventually, the US Department of Justice ruled that the school needed to change its dress code to accommodate the wearing of religious clothing. The Pluralism Project at Harvard University engages students in studying the new religious diversity in the United States.

As you read, consider the following questions:

1. How many Sikhs are mentioned as living in France?
2. What percentage of the French population favored the ban?
3. What grade was the student from Muskogee, Oklahoma in when she was suspended twice?

The French Ban

In December 2003, French President Jacques Chirac announced that Muslim headscarves, Jewish skullcaps, and large crosses were to be banned in French public schools, arguing that he intended

"Controversy over the Headscarf (2004)," The Pluralism Project at Harvard University. Reprinted with permission.

to uphold the principle of secularism, which is the "pillar of the French Constitution." Though the decree was directed towards Muslim, Jewish, and Christian religious articles, critics argued that it specifically targeted France's growing Muslim immigrant community. Chirac's announcement set off an international controversy regarding the separation of church and state and the individual right to freedom of expression, prompting responses not only from throughout Europe but in the United States and the Middle East. In March, when the French parliament approved the ban with 276 votes in favor and 20 against, studies showed that about 70% of the French population favored the ban as well as most of France's political parties.

International Response

International response to the French ban was swift. In December, John Hanford, the Bush Administration's top ranking official on religious reform, stated that "all persons should be able to practice their religions peacefully, without government interference." (NYT, Dec 18). Demonstrators against the ban rallied in London, Cairo, Beirut, and San Francisco, and in Paris, thousands of Muslim women marched through the streets chanting "The veil, my choice!" In Iraq, Shiite clerics called for a boycott of French products in protest of the ban. It was also unclear as to how the ban would affect the status of France's 6,000 Sikhs, and in January, 2-3,000 Sikhs came from throughout Europe to march in Paris' Place de la Republique. Soon after, over 45 members of the U.S. Congress wrote to the French government to express their concern, arguing that the ban would force French children to choose between their faith and their schooling. The ban is set to take affect in French public schools in September, 2004.

The German Ban and the Italian Controversy

In October, a decision by Germany's highest court to allow Muslim teacher Fereshta Ludin to wear her headscarf to work as long as no state laws prohibited it prompted the majority of German states to begin planning to pass such laws. In December, German Chancellor Gerhard Schroder spoke against allowing public school teachers to wear the hijab, saying that Islamic dress has "no place" among German's civil servants. (The Scotsman, Dec.22). On April 1, 2003 the conservative German state Baden'Wuerttemberg became the first German state to ban teachers from wearing Muslim headscarves in the classroom, and in December Bavaria, Germany's biggest state, began drafting a similar law with the aim of protecting pupils against "fundamentalist influences" (Dec. 9, BBC News). By March, six German states in Germany had banned the headscarf, including the city-state Berlin. Meanwhile, a kindergarten teacher in Italy was asked to remove her headscarf in March because it might "frighten children," prompting an international debate on the role of Muslims in a predominantly Catholic society.

The Oklahoma Headscarf Controversy

The subject of headscarves in the classroom also made headlines in the United States this year. In October, Nashala Hearn, an 11 year-old sixth grader at Ben Franklin Science academy in Muskogee, Oklahoma, was suspended twice for wearing a Muslim headscarf to school. School officials argued that the hijab violated school dress codes, which prohibited students from wearing "hats, caps, bandanna, plastic caps, hoods or jackets" due to gang-related activities. The Rutherford Institute, a Virginia based civil liberties Institute, filed a suit on Hearsts' behalf, arguing that the school violated her right to free speech and religious expression. In October, the First Amendment Center memorably argued in an editorial: "In France today, a Muslim girl must remove her head scarf if she wants to attend a public school. And in Germany, efforts are under way to ban the hijab from schools and in the workplace… in the United States, it should be un-American to make someone take it off." On May 19 the Justice Department announced that the Muskogee Public School District must change its dress code to allow for religious clothing.

In the United States Hijabs Lead to Social Obstacles for Women

Tom Gjelten

In the following viewpoint, Tom Gjelten argues that Muslim women in America have different experiences wearing headscarves in public, and most are not positive. The author interviews several American Muslim women, who offer their personal views. In one account, a woman says that it was a lot easier for her to make friends before she started wearing her hijab and that the head cover served as an obstacle for her. In another account, a lawyer stopped wearing her hijab because it interfered with her work. Gjelten covers issues of religion, faith, and belief for NPR News.

As you read, consider the following questions:

1. At what college did the Christian professor Larycia Hawkins work?
2. What is the name of the woman who stopped wearing her hijab because it was interfering with her work as a lawyer?
3. What major newspaper published an op-ed asking non-Muslim women not to wear headscarves?

For Muslim women, a headscarf—or hijab—is a visible sign of their faith and identity, and whether to wear one is a big decision. The recent decision by a Christian college professor to don

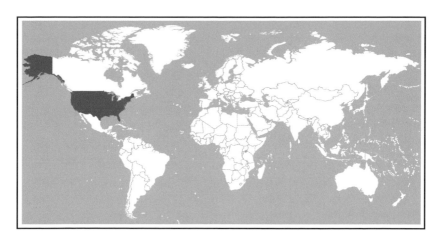

a headscarf out of solidarity with her Muslim sisters highlighted the hijab question, at least for non-Muslims. For Muslim women themselves, especially in the United States, it was an old story.

"Before I wore hijab, making friends with people who weren't Muslim was a lot easier," says Maryam Adamu, who was born in North Carolina to immigrants from Nigeria. Before she began wearing a headscarf three years ago, people didn't know she was Muslim—until she told them.

"I, like, Trojan-horsed my Islam," she says, laughing. "Like, 'You're already my friend. I know you like me. Now you know I'm Muslim, and you're going to learn about this faith.' " Once she started wearing a headscarf, she encountered a social obstacle she hadn't seen before. "Now, I have to work a lot harder to get into people's lives who aren't Muslim," she says.

For some women, that can be a burden. Asma Uddin, born in Miami to Pakistani parents, is devout in her religious beliefs, but she stopped wearing a headscarf when she found it interfering with her work as a lawyer.

"I was tired of being a political spokesperson for my faith," she says. "I felt that I should be able to put that away, and wearing a headscarf in public doesn't give you that luxury. I was tired of trying to prove that Muslim women in headscarves are also empowered, [by saying] 'Look at me. I'm working in a white-shoe law firm with a headscarf on.' Uddin is a now a staff attorney for the Becket Fund for Religious Liberty.

The hijab question took on new significance in the aftermath of the decision by Wheaton College professor Larycia Hawkins to wear a hijab out of sympathy for Muslim women who feel marginalized by their headscarves. Soon after that, Asra Nomani, who describes herself as a Muslim reformer, co-wrote a provocative op-ed in the *Washington Post* asking non-Muslim women not to wear headscarves, even in solidarity, because in her judgment it stands for "an interpretation of Islam we reject."

"The headscarf has become a political symbol for an ideology of Islam that is exported to the world by the theocracies of the governments of Iran and Saudi Arabia," she told NPR.

The commentary provoked an outcry among "hijabi" Muslim women in the United States, many of whom bristled at the suggestion that wearing a headscarf signals their submission to a conservative Islamic ideology.

"I support women who choose to wear it [and] who choose not to wear it," says Yasmin Elhady, a civil rights attorney who was born in Egypt and raised in Alabama. "I don't believe that anyone should comment on why women should wear it or shouldn't wear it. I think that if women want to wear it ... we should be supportive of them."

The controversy over Nomani's commentary was reinforced when the *New York Times* last month hosted an online debate on the question, "Do Non-Muslims Help or Hurt Women by Wearing Hijabs?" with Nomani's viewpoint included.

Dalia Mogahed, born in Wisconsin to parents from Egypt, didn't even like the question. As research director of the Institute for Social Policy and Understanding, she focuses on the American Muslim community.

"Some Muslim women wear hijab, some don't, and it's just not an issue," she says. "It's a non-issue. But then you have one person write an engaging article, and suddenly it's a debate that we're supposed to be having, [a debate] that we are not having."

Periodical and Internet Sources Bibliography

The following articles have been selected to supplement the diverse views presented in this chapter.

Lila Abu-Lughod, "Do Muslim Women Need Saving?" Time, November 1, 2013. http://ideas.time.com/2013/11/01/do-muslim-women-need-saving/

Yvonne Aburrow, "Should Public Expressions of Religion Be Allowed?" Patheos, Feb. 11, 2016, http://www.patheos.com/blogs/sermonsfromthemound/2016/02/should-public-expressions-of-religion-be-allowed/.

BBC News, "The Islamic Veil Across Europe, BBC, January 31, 2017, http://www.bbc.com/news/world-europe-13038095.

The Economist, "Why the French Are So Strict About Islamic Head Coverings," July 7, 2014. https://www.economist.com/blogs/economist-explains/2014/07/economist-explains-2

Peter Hopkins, "Five truths about the hijab that need to be told," The Conversation, August 18, 2016, https://theconversation.com/five-truths-about-the-hijab-that-need-to-be-told-63892.

Radhika Sanghani , "Burka bans: The countries where Muslim women can't wear veils," The Telegraph, August 17, 2017, http://www.telegraph.co.uk/women/life/burka-bans-the-countries-where-muslim-women-cant-wear-veils/.

Leland Ware, "No Headscarves in Schools, No Burqas in Public: Colorblind Racism in France," Huffington Post, July 3, 2014, https://www.huffingtonpost.com/leland-ware/burqa-ban france_b_5555732.html.

Matthew Weaver, "Burqa bans, headscarves and veils: a timeline of legislation in the west," The Guardian, March 14, 2017, https://www.theguardian.com/world/2017/mar/14/headscarves-and muslim-veil-ban-debate-timeline.

CHAPTER 2

Women and Religious Clothing in Public Spaces

In India Religious Attire Is a Restriction by the Patriarchy

Nikita Azad

In the following viewpoint, Nikita Azad argues that the debate about religious clothing should focus on women in particular. The author questions whether dress codes within religions are actually part of the religion or culture, or if they are a way for the patriarchy to dominate women. It is no secret that men's religious clothing is typically more lenient than that of women, and the garb instituted on women is designed to cover certain parts of their body because it may draw attention to them or incite sexual feelings in the men who see them. Azad finishes the article by talking about changing society and getting further away from patriarchy. Azad is a student and gender rights activist.

As you read, consider the following questions:

1. In which city in India did an engineering college give orders to women that leggings, tight pants and tops, and short kurtis are not allowed on the campus?
2. What is patriarchy?
3. What would lead to women being branded as "loose?"

2015 was a year of oppression and resistance, exploitation and revolts, demons and dreams. While on one hand, we were faceted with a strong Brahaminical fundamentalism, on the other,

"Dress Codes: Culture or Patriarchy?" by Nikita Azad, Countercurrents.org, January 5, 2016. Reprinted by permission.

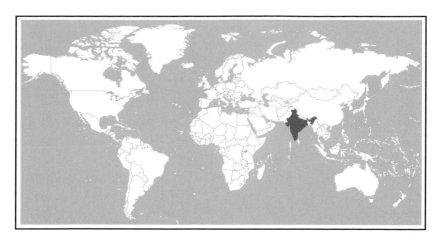

we created a strong communal harmony. While on one hand, we were mocked as aliens for our sexuality, on the other, we celebrated Queers. While on one hand, our homes were demolished in the name of beauty, on the other, we pledged to own our homes, our factories, our products. Where the state planned to sell higher education to WTO, and we said in huge numbers 'Occupy UGC' and 'WTO Go Back'. 2015 was the year where we were preached that menstruation is a sin, but we said #happytobleed, doing away with all taboos that restrict our mobility.

With all the resistances that we put last year, we entered into a new year, pledging and hoping to make and see a better, egalitarian, just society. We welcomed 2016 to life, love, and struggle. But, while many people were still celebrating the New Year, we were given another gift on the very first day of New Year.

On January 1, 2016, many pilgrims had gone to various temples in Tamil Nadu to seek blessings from god for the next year, where women were turned back, and sent home for wearing western clothes, jeans, or shorts. It happened because in December the Madras High Court ordered temple authorities in Tamil Nadu state to refuse entry to anyone wearing jeans, bermuda shorts, skirts, short-sleeves or tight leggings to "enhance spiritual ambiance." Earlier in 2015, Prayar Gopalakrishnan, head of Devaswom Committee, Sabarimala Temple, Kerala had given another controversial statement that once a 'purity' checking machine (that checks whether women are menstruating or not) is invented, he will think about letting women enter the temple. Also, Mr. Abubacker, a leader of Sunni sect of Muslims said that gender equality is a myth, and women are fit only for reproduction. Continuing the legacy of patriarchy, women were given another archaic diktat which would control the amount of clothes they would put on their body.

Although Madras High Court dictated a dress code for men also, i.e. formal pants and shirt, or dhoti etc, but the scenario in the society at large is anti-women, which is why I choose to address the question from the lens of patriarchy. Secondly, the dress code that men were obliged to follow doesn't include the 'decent-indecent' conflict; rather they are merely expected to look 'sober'. Whereas when it comes to women, a lot of arguments are given like such clothes which reveal conventionally hidden parts of female body might distract the attention of people, incite sexual feelings, make women 'astray' i.e. break the sexual barriers imposed by society. Also, this isn't the first time such a statement has come; thus we must see it in continuity rather than spontaneity. On November 23, 2015 the committee of Kashi Vishwanath temple gave a diktat that foreigners, or women who wear 'revealing' dresses will not be allowed entry, and also the temple placed 25 sarees at its entry point for them to change! Earlier in October, 2012 women wearing jeans were banned from entering Jain temples in Madhya Pradesh.

The relation of women with clothes has always been an issue of debate in society, from where the sexual nature of society is judged. If in a society, women do not cover their bodies from head to toe, do not wear bras regularly, etc, they are branded as 'loose women', and society is recognised as one promoting 'promiscuity'. But, if women cover their bodies fully, they are referred to as 'decent', 'homely' etc, and society is called 'closed', or 'well civilized'. However, this branding varies as we change the sample of judges, but in Indian context, this is the most appropriate categorization of societies, and women. Clothes have also become a symbol of societies, whereby we recognise societies, classes, castes by their clothes without interacting with people, and without knowing their profession. Clothes not only reflect economic condition of individual, but also social status, social acceptance, and social relations. We identify different cultures from the clothes they wear, rather than thoughts they bear. For example, if an individual wearing sturdy leaves or animal skin is shown to us, the first identity to which we relate the individual is Adivasi. The jungle, their dance, their music, even their faces, do not matter, but only their clothes. This is the level up to which clothes and culture are intertwined.

It is quite amazing how a thing of need, clothes, which humans invented to cover their bodies, became a tool of division among the very humans. The invention of agriculture, development of productive forces, private ownership of animals, slaves, and finally land, paved way for the transition from matriarchal society to a patriarchal one. The urge of major owners of means of production (man) to transfer the ownership to their legitimate children required a strict discipline on sexual nature of women. The first monogamy was imposed on women, to get a legitimate heir to the land of father. From this sexual control, started the first cultural manifestations of patriarchy in ideologies that preached that women are subordinate to men in every respect, and are fit only for homely purposes. Many justifications were created in order to counter every resistance, and question, which included developing an inferiority complex within a female with respect to her own body. She was excluded from direct production processes, and made to perform household functions. Most importantly, the work she did in home was perceived as her duty, not as labour, while 'work' meant labour that men did beyond the realm of home. However this strictness was more practiced in land-owning classes, whereas in landless classes, there was certain flexibility. This was also because the sexual availability of lower class-caste women was at the discretion of upper class-caste men. Lower class-caste women were considered as objects of manual labour, as well as sexual labour. Within this structure, clothing was decided. Where on one hand, women were forced to remain within homes, cover themselves up completely; on the other hand, Dalit women were forced to make multiple sexual relations with men from the upper castes. This hypocrisy is manifested in the tradition of 19th century Travancore where lower caste women (Nadar climbers) were not allowed to cover their bosoms to punctuate their low status.

The reason why I am placing these arguments historically is that today when fundamentalists talk about 'preserving our culture', maintaining 'spiritual ambience', and regulate the behaviour of women, they tend to hide the heinous oppression in their very 'Great Indian Culture'. The statement of Madras high court said that western clothes are inappropriate for a place like temple, but stripping Dalit women naked, making them run naked over a donkey, raping them to 'remind' them of their status, is far more inappropriate, and a great threat to our plural culture. On May 15, 2015 four dalit women were stripped naked in the middle of the village by upper castes because a girl of upper caste had eloped with a boy from a dalit family. Later on August 19, 2015, khap panchayat of Baghpat village, Meerut ordered that a dalit woman and her sister be raped because their brother had eloped with a woman of upper caste. Facts state that 21 dalit women are raped each week, and many a times, rapes are celebrated as victories in wars, as assertion of rights.

Temples, which are exhibited as pride of the nation, were made only for upper castes, whereby all Dalit were refrained from going in. Till date, menstruating women cannot go into temples in the name of culture and tradition. Moreover, temples which are viewed as places of virtue are also perpetrators of crimes. In these very temples, women were married to deities and forced to have sex with priests under the Devadasi Pratha. On 26 October, 2015 a 10-year old girl was raped by a priest in a temple in Faridabad, and earlier on May 2, 2015 a woman was raped in temple premises by a priest. Such anti-women, sexist atmosphere of temples, and Casteist, patriarchal priests have absolutely no right to decide what a woman wears and what not. The priests who justify gender oppression as an extension of nature, as a gift of God, have no authority to dictate whether a man, or woman, or transgender enters a temple, or not.

The question, here, is not about entering the temple, but about putting restrictions on a woman's behaviour, routine as well as sexual in the name of culture. This is not just patriarchal, but also political. Regulating women's choices is the politics of maintaining the classist-castiest-patriarchal power relations. Diktats regarding clothes, hostel timings, night outs, relationships, sex, are not given because men have a special psychology, but because the state structure and corporates need patriarchy to extract maximum profit from the labour of masses. The state makes one section of toiling masses, men, to stand against another, women, by propagating, and instilling patriarchy through various ideological and coercive apparatuses, and makes the loot easier for itself. Relating women to 'honour' and secluding them from public places is the biggest politics that state has ever done with its people. By doing this, it has made half the population, a mere spectator of state's policies and crimes, which is celebrated as 'decency' of women by another half.

Within this context, comes the attitude of temples, colleges, workplaces and other institutions. On 21 September, 2015 an engineering college in Chennai gave orders to women that leggings, tight pants and tops, lose hair hairdo, short kurtis etc are not allowed within the campus. This system of making choices for women is very deep-rooted, and we need to look at it comprehensively and historically to find the correct answers and solutions. This is not the first time a temple has given such a diktat, but this is not even the last. We need to find ways by which we can change society, by which we can break the internalization of patriarchy within the minds of women. We need to address the questions of caste, class, gender with an embracing intersectionality, and forge a struggle against oppressive structures with a correct ideological basis.

Meanwhile, I would like to say, that this year is also going to be a struggling one for us, for masses.

In Britain Muslim Women Don't See the Hijab As a Symbol of Oppression

Pina Sadar

In the following viewpoint Pina Sadar argues that the hijab recently has become a symbol of many negative things in western culture, including the oppression of women in Islam. However, many young Muslim women identify as feminists and are intent on fighting for their rights, including the right to wear a hijab. These women are often caught in between two cultures and misunderstood, and they emphasize that less attention should be paid to the attire of Muslim women and more should be paid to other rights, such as education and health. The author calls into question the right of westerners to speak on behalf of Muslim women. Sadar is a PhD candidate in Anthropology at Durham University.

As you read, consider the following questions:

1. What does the author credit for FIFA lifting its ban on hijabs?
2. For whose rights does the Safra Project advocate?
3. What work does the street artist known as Princess Hijab do?

T errorism, oppression, fundamentalism and victimhood are only a few of the buzzwords that inevitably accompany discussions about Islamic headgear. From burqa-bans to atrocities against women in some Islamic countries, the veil is frequently

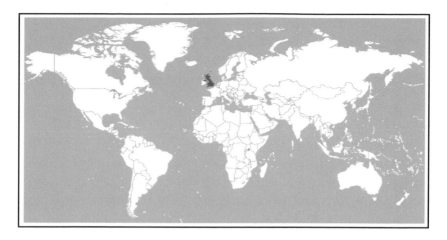

framed as a piece of cloth imposed on an individual by her religion and culture.

But beyond the oft-peddled static images of oppressed and depressed Muslim women, the reality is far more dynamic. In multicultural Britain in particular, women of all ages, ethnicities and economic backgrounds purposefully don the hijab. Many see it as an important element of a modern Muslim female identity.

Although the hijab essentially conveys deeply religious sentiments, its meanings stretch beyond spirituality. Influenced by political and social changes, the Islamic headscarf reflects the eclectic lifestyles and the beliefs of women who embrace it. Some wear it to reaffirm their ethnic belonging and others to manifest their disagreement with British military interventions in Muslim countries.

While many think connecting Islam with feminism is an impossible contradiction, a generation of young British Muslim women feels a strong need to promote its rights in public. These women want to dismantle patriarchy in Islam and beyond. And they want to wear a headscarf while they do it.

Hijab 2.0

Burgeoning feminist movements are especially vocal online. Just like many other social movements in the 21st century, women are using social media in particular to address gender inequalities in society.

Their digital activism is proving effective. In September 2013, Birmingham College reversed its face veil ban after a Twitter outcry that argued for a woman's right to choose her attire. Similarly, online campaigners played a part in pressuring FIFA to lift its ban on hijabs on the football field.

The recently trending Twitter hashtag #lifeofamuslimfeminist is an example of the growing popularity of online Muslim feminism. Twitter user Noorulann Shahid told the Feminist Times that she started the hashtag because she wanted to explain the frustration of being a Muslim feminist "navigating between Muslims telling you that you don't need feminism and mainstream feminism rejecting you." Shahid argued, "when this happens, there is nowhere you can position yourself comfortably."

Her idea snowballed and the hashtag is now attached to thousands of tweets capturing the challenges and aspirations associated with being a Muslim feminist. They are often closely related to experiences of wearing the hijab.

"If only men obsessed over the education, health and justice of Muslim women like they obsess over hijab," tweets one women. Another user adds: "Getting lectures on how your hijab isn't 'correct' by brother who clearly missed the memo about lowering your gaze."

By publicly discussing their veils and the double standards men often exhibit when they try to control how women dress, these Twitter users are reasserting their right to shape the meaning of their own clothes. Social media channels help them to voice opinions that would normally remain ignored by the mainstream media.

The LBTQ Hijab

In addition to general online discussions about Islamic feminism, Muslim queer movements are also seeking to reconcile their relationship with veils.

Some celebrate the hijab as an emblem of female inclusivity. The Safra Project, a group that advocates for lesbian, bisexual, queer and transgender Muslim women's rights is one. It claims hijabs and burqas are part of a Muslim woman's queer identity.

Its members want to embrace their sexual identity with the help of Islam rather than be forced to choose between the two.

Organisations such as Safra are, however, aware that their attitude is not commonly accepted and shared. On one side they face strong criticism from Muslims and on the other they are excluded by non-Muslim queers too.

Muslim queers often feel that their visibly Islamic outfits are not welcome in LGBTQ circles. Even those who are often subjected to similar discrimination themselves frequently fail to understand that the veil does not correspond with narrow gender and sexual identities.

The Anti-capitalist Hijab

The hijab has long been debated in connection to Islamic gender roles, but some headscarf wearers are using it to reflect on modern British ones too. In her *Guardian* column, publicist Nadiya Takolia, who adopted the hijab after delving into feminism, remarks:

> This is not about protection from men's lusts. It is me telling the world that my femininity is not available for public consumption. I am taking control of it, and I don't want to be part of a system that reduces and demeans women.

The same message is captured creatively in the work of Princess Hijab. This controversial French street artist "hijabizes" sexualised subway advertisements by painting the Islamic veil over images of bikini-clad models. Just like Nadiya Takolia, she sends out a clear message—women's bodies are not for sale.

With real and painted veils, women reject the sexualisation of female bodies by covering them. They gain a sense of self-respect without adhering to capitalist norms of beauty. They promote a new version of feminism.

Democratic discussions about veiling are welcome but ultimately the public needs to acknowledge a woman's freedom to choose not only her own form of a dress but also to shape its meanings—whatever they may be.

In France Secularism Leads to a Ban on Burqas

Raza Habib Raja

In the following viewpoint, Raza Habib Raja argues that the burqa and niqab ban in France that was upheld by the European Court of Human Rights was based on France's own brand of secularism, which does not blend with liberalism sufficiently. Raja digs deeper into the ban, bringing up the fact that the ban has shed light on ideas like secularism and multiculturalism. The author writes that the French model of secularism does not restrict the separation of state and religion nationwide but that it does extend to some areas of the public. Raja is a writer and Ph.D. student in political science and government.

As you read, consider the following questions:

1. How many women does the ban affect?
2. How many supporting votes did the "secularity law" receive when it passed in 2004?
3. What is secularism?

I n a landmark judgment, the European Court of Human Rights has upheld a ban by France on wearing the Muslim full-face veil — the niqab.

According to the press release of the court judgment:

"Burqah Ban, Multiculturalism and Secularism," by Raza Habib Raja, Raza Habib Raja, September 8, 2014. Reprinted by permission.

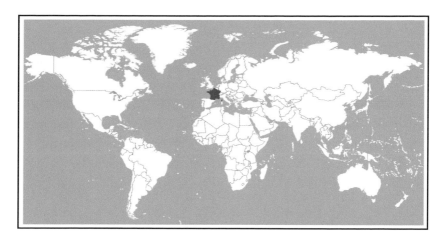

The European Court of Human Rights held by a majority, that there had been no violation of Article 8 (right to respect for private and family life) of the European Convention on Human Rights, and no violation of Article 9 (right to respect for freedom of thought, conscience and religion);unanimously, that there had been no violation of Article 14 (prohibition of discrimination) of the European Convention combined with Articles 8 or 9.

Further, the Court also endorsed the stance taken by the government that the ban encouraged "living together" as face played an important role in social interaction. Moreover, the Court also admitted that while the ban affects certain Muslim women but at the same time there are no restrictions to wear items of clothing (even in accordance with religion) which do not conceal the face. Thus, the ban imposed is not based on the supposed religious symbolism but on the fact that veil covers the face.

It has to be noted that while imposing the ban, the government had also made "security of the society" as one of the justifications. However, at the time of imposition also it was argued by many that security was not the only concern and factors like cultural differences between Muslims and the West and the French need to show commitment to secularism were the actual reasons.

It has been argued and with justification that the veil issue is not merely restricted to security (though that is also an integral part) but is part of a wider debate about multiculturalism in Europe, as many feel that ethnic and religious minorities should be assimilated properly.

The ban has actually spurred an interesting debate on the very nature of ideas like secularism, multiculturalism, religious freedom and liberalism. While the ban was expected to be supported by rightwing elements, the interesting thing was that the ban actually resulted in the division of liberal opinion as well. The liberals became polarized and became divided into two camps and continue to be like that.

According to one group, Burqah symbolizes religious oppression of women and is a relic of medieval times and therefore completely out of place in the Western world and particularly France which is a proud secular republic. Moreover, they also supplement their argument that if someone immigrant is not comfortable then he/she should leave France. Their argument is further augmented by the fact that France bans all explicit religious symbols in public schools. In fact, in 2004, the new "secularity law" was passed with overwhelming support and a vote of 276 to 20. It bans the wearing of Muslim hijabs, Sikh's head coverings, large Christian crosses or crucifixes, Jewish yarmulkes, etc.

In short, French model of secularism does not restrict separation of state and religion to statecraft alone but extends it to some areas of public sphere as well.

The opposing group argues that secularism is by its essence separation of state and religion and at the same time it espouses religious freedom. If religious symbols and for that matter practices do not infringe upon the rights of others, then these should be allowed. Secularism according to them is not negation of religious freedom in the public sphere but rather separation of religion from the state. When liberalism is also thrown in, then the issue becomes even more critical because liberalism by its orientation advocates freedom provided it is not harmful to others. According to them, if a woman is wearing a veil out of her own choice and is not compelled by the society then despite

Hijab: Veiled in Controversy

Hijab is an Islamic concept of modesty and privacy. This concept is not unique to Islam, but embraced by other religions, such as Judaism (where the concept of modesty is called Tzuniut) and Christianity. The Islamic concept of hijab is most often expressed in women's clothing. Hijab garments range from simple head scarves (called khimaar or simply hijab) to head-to-toe cloaks such as abayas and burqas. This photo gallery illustrates some of the many types of hijab clothing.

Although firmly rooted in Islamic tradition, hijab is not strictly defined in the Muslim holy book, the Quran. It is often a personal and cultural concept, not a religious one. Expression of hijab varies within the Muslim world and beyond. These verses of the Quran offer insight into hijab and relevant ideas about modesty, respect, privacy, and humility: Chapter 24, verses 30 and 31; Chapter 33, verses 32 and 33; and Chapter 33, verses 53 and 54.

Public expression of hijab is a very controversial issue. It is, first and foremost, an act of worship among Muslim women. In the United States, wearing hijab clothing is a right guaranteed by the First Amendment—as freedom of speech and freedom of religion. However, hijab clothing has also become a potent indicator of identity, with many non-Muslims viewing it as a political statement. Some communities interpret hijab as a sign of Islamic fundamentalism, the refusal of immigrants to integrate into mainstream society, or the oppression of women.

Governments address hijab coverings in different ways. Some restrict wearing any religious clothing, including hijab, in public. Two nations (Saudi Arabia and Iran) require women to wear hijab coverings. Most nations do not have either restrictions or requirements concerning hijab clothing.

"Hijab: Veiled in Controversy," by Caryl-Sue, National Geographic Society, February 11, 2013.

the apparent religiosity of Burqah and its historical symbolic association with oppression in some countries, she should be allowed to wear it. Just because Taliban have forced women to wear Burqah in Afghanistan does not mean that a woman in France is also being forced.

Moreover, many critics also point that such bans have less to do with "gender equality" or emancipation but are rather reflective of rising racism. In fact, bringing these issues into needless controversy like Burqah which do not infringe upon freedom of others, merely increases xenophobia.

It is an interesting ethical dilemma where both the camps are busy indulging in name calling.

I think this debate is one of the most interesting one and needs deliberation without needless name calling. Because it is not just Burqah but the nature of secularism, which is under scrutiny.

First, I would like to acknowledge and admit that France is a sovereign country and has its own interpretation of secularism. It is fiercely protective about its version of secularism and there is an overwhelming consensus within the population about it. Moreover, at least on the face of it, the French have not intentionally discriminated against Muslims as they have similar yardsticks for other religious symbols also. French law on secularity and conspicuous religious symbols in schools which was passed in 2004 banned explicit religious symbols Prohibited items included headscarves for Muslim girls, yarmulkes for Jewish boys, and turbans for Sikh boys.

However, even then the most controversial element was the ban on hijab (or scarf). It was noted even then that although it was apparently neutral but the burden eventually fell rather disproportionally on Muslim girls.

Another issue is that Muslims are more sensitive when it comes to their religion. Let's not forget that the ban on full face veil actually affects less than 2,000 women and yet it is evoking a strong response.

Personally, I do not think that French have discriminated against Muslims intentionally; it is their interpretation of secularism coupled with the fact that a full face veil has been common in those countries where women are treated as a mere commodity.

The association of full face veil with oppression of women is extremely strong and may have had a strong influence in shaping up the bill which banned such veils. Apparently French have their reasons and within the context of their own interpretation of secularism, they have not done an inconsistent thing. So the allegation that they are merely discriminatory against Muslims is at least debatable.

However, having said so I would also like to add that I personally do not agree with French model of secularism though I acknowledge their right to impose it in their own country. I think that secularism has to blend in with liberalism. French model of secularism is not essentially liberal at least when it comes to religious beliefs. I would rather prefer the US model which is liberal as well as secular when it comes to religion. The U.S. Bills of Rights and particularly the First Amendment are excellent examples of how to achieve a very delicate balance between religious freedom and secularism.

I think use of religious symbols provided these do not infringe upon the freedom of others, should be allowed. If a woman is willingly wearing Burqah, (and in Western countries majority of those who wear Burqah, do so out of choice) then she should be allowed. Yes veil may have been a symbol of oppression in some countries but symbols assume relevance according to the circumstances. A full veil in Afghanistan may be a forced thing but a veil in Europe is less likely to be the same thing. And if a veil is being forced in Europe then being an open society with better human right record, the woman has full recourse to law and state's protection.

The same goes with the need for assimilation. As the world becomes more cosmopolitan and West continues to get more immigrants, the need for assimilation has to be fulfilled smartly and with due precaution. An act, which is restricted to just one's own self, such as wearing a veil, has to be differentiated with an act which infringes on the freedom of thought, expression and security of others. I personally think USA does a much better job than several European countries.

Secularism has to blend in with religious freedom and tolerance and only then it can be a true liberal version of secularism. The

French brand of secularism will not make the concept of secularism popular and will not work in a pluralistic society. It will rather defame and further intensify the confusions surrounding the concept of secularism. This is not to suggest that Muslim countries have credible record compared to France when it comes to minorities as they fare much much worse but at the same time it does raise a question whether France's secular model is the optimal approach towards achieving a delicate balance between religious freedom and secularism.

Let's not forget that French laws have been criticized by Human Rights Watch and other organizations also. For example, the Human Rights Watch had the following opinion about the 2004 French law on secularity and conspicuous religious symbols:

> The proposed French law banning Islamic headscarves and other visible religious symbols in state schools would violate the rights to freedom of religion and expression. Under international law, states can only limit religious practices when there is a compelling public safety reason, when the manifestation of religious beliefs would impinge on the rights of others, or when it serves a legitimate educational function (such as prohibiting practices that preclude student-teacher interaction). Muslim headscarves, Sikh turbans, Jewish skullcaps and large Christian crosses—which are among the visible religious symbols that would be prohibited—do not pose a threat to public health, order or morals; they have no effect on the fundamental rights and freedoms of other students; and they do not undermine a school's educational function.

As the globe becomes more cosmopolitan, it becomes even more important to get our balance right. And a correct balance is what underpins liberal secularism.

The Majority of Countries Restrict Women's Religious Attire

Pew Research Center

In the following viewpoint, the Pew Research Center presents an annual study that looks at government restrictions on religion in addition to social hostilities driven by religion. Overall, the study reveals that there are more countries that restrict women's ability to wear religious clothing than countries that require women to dress a specific way. For example, Iraq, Libya, Saudi Arabia and Sudan all have laws requiring women to wear religious clothing. The Pew Research Center is a nonpartisan fact tank that conducts extensive polling and research to inform the public about the issues, attitudes and trends shaping America and the world.

As you read, consider the following questions:

1. How many countries of the 198 total studied had at least one law regulating women's religious attire in 2012 and 2013?

2. What percentage of European countries had at least one such restriction on women's religious clothing in 2012–2013?

3. More than how many countries had at least one incident involving harassment against women due to religious clothing in 2013?

"Restrictions on Women's Religious Attire" Pew Research Center, Washington, DC (April 2016) http://www.pewforum.org/2016/04/05/restrictions-on-womens-religious-attire/. Reprinted by permission.

In many countries around the world, women's choices about their attire and appearance are restricted to some degree by government laws, policies or regulations. In recent years, most of these countries have had laws or policies that ban women from wearing religious attire in public places or limit their ability to do so in some circumstances. By comparison, far fewer countries require women to wear particular types of attire (such as headscarves or long dresses) for religious reasons.

As part of its annual study on government restrictions on religion and social hostilities involving religion, Pew Research Center tracks the number of countries where some level of government – national, provincial or local – regulates "the wearing of religious symbols, such as head coverings for women and facial hair for men."[1] Looking at only those laws, policies or regulations that apply specifically to women, the Center finds that 50 of the 198 countries and territories included in the study had at least one law or policy regulating women's religious attire in 2012 and 2013, the two most recent years for which data are available. About three-quarters of those countries (39 of the 50, or 78%) had a law or policy limiting women's ability to wear religious attire, while about a quarter (12 of the 50, or 24%) had at least one law or policy requiring women to wear particular attire. Some of these laws or policies applied nationwide, while others were imposed at the provincial, state or local level. One country – Russia – had policies forbidding women from wearing religious attire (in the territory of Stavropol, where Muslim headscarves, or hijabs, were banned in public schools) as well as policies requiring women to wear religious attire (in Chechnya, where women were required to wear hijabs in all public buildings).[2]

Laws or policies limiting women's ability to wear religious attire were particularly common in Europe, where 18 of the region's 45 countries (40%) had at least one such restriction in 2012-2013.[3] Several European countries effectively banned certain types of religious garb in public places. In France, for example, authorities continued to enforce a law passed in 2010 that prohibits people from covering their faces in public places, including government buildings, public transportation and venues such as restaurants and movie theaters. Those who did not comply with a police officer's request to uncover their face could be fined or ordered to attend a citizenship class.[4] A similar policy was in effect in Belgium, where police continued to enforce a 2011 federal law banning people from wearing clothing that covers the face, or large parts of it, in public places. Violators could be fined and/or detained for up to seven days.[5] In December 2012, Belgium's Constitutional Court upheld the ban, ruling that it was necessary to protect public safety, ensure equality between men and women and preserve "a certain conception of 'living together' in society."[6]

In the Middle East and North Africa, four countries – Iraq, Libya, Saudi Arabia and Sudan – had laws requiring women to wear religious attire. Authorities in Saudi Arabia, for instance, continued to require women to wear an abaya (a loose-fitting black cloak) in public.[7] Four Middle Eastern countries (20%) – Algeria, Egypt, Israel and Oman – had policies limiting women's ability to wear religious attire in at least some situations. In Egypt, for example, the government banned female employees of the national airline from wearing hijabs at work until 2012.[8] Security forces in Israel prevented some Palestinian women prisoners from wearing hijabs during interrogations.[9] In Algeria, female government workers were allowed to wear headscarves and face-covering Islamic veils (niqabs), but authorities discouraged certain employees from doing so if it would "complicate the performance of their official duties."[10. See U.S. Department of State. May 20, 2013. "Algeria." 2012 Report on International Religious Freedom.] Oman allowed women to wear headscarves in official photographs, but it did not allow them to wear face-covering veils.[10]

In the Asia-Pacific region, laws or policies requiring women to wear religious attire were found in six of the 50 countries (12%). In Indonesia, for example, 79 local bylaws required women to wear a hijab in 2013,[12. See Human Rights Watch. 2014. "World Report 2014: Indonesia.] while Iranian women were required to cover their hair and wear loose-fitting clothing in public places.11 Laws restricting women's ability to wear religious attire were present in 11 of the 50 countries in the Asia-Pacific region (22%) in 2012-2013. In India, some schools and colleges in certain areas banned Muslim female students and teachers from wearing headscarves, citing uniform dress codes.[14. See U.S. Department of State. May 20, 2013. "India." 2012 Report on International Religious Freedom. Also see July 17, 2012. "'Hijab May Affect Academic Process, Make Others Uncomfortable." *The Express Tribune.*] Singapore, meanwhile, prohibited some public-sector employees, including nurses, front-line military officers and employees of certain schools, from wearing hijabs in the workplace.[15. See U.S. Department of State. July 28, 2014. "Singapore." 2013 Report on International Religious Freedom. Also see Nov. 13, 2013. "Singapore: Campaigners Bid to Overturn Hijab Ban." *BBC News.*]

In sub-Saharan Africa, laws or policies requiring women to wear religious attire were present in one country – Somalia – where the Islamic extremist group al-Shabaab required women living in areas under its control to be veiled while in public in 2012[12] Laws or policies restricting religious attire were present in five countries in sub-Saharan Africa. Women in Mozambique were not allowed to wear headscarves in official photographs for identification documents, and girls were prohibited from wearing face-covering veils or body-covering burqas in public schools.[13] In Kenya, some government schools prevented girls from attending classes if they wore headscarves or other religious attire. This policy affected not only Muslims but also members of the Akorino group, which combines Christian and traditional African styles of worship; its followers, both men and women, usually cover their heads.[18. See U.S. Department of State. July 28, 2014. "Kenya." 2013 Report on International Religious Freedom. Also see Namlola, Juma. March 25, 2015. "Muslim Leaders to Appeal High Court Ban on Veils in Schools." *The Nation.*]

The sources used for this study did not detect any countries in the Americas that required women to wear religious dress in 2012-2013, but one country – Canada – restricted women's religious attire. Candidates for Canadian citizenship had to remove any face-covering veils when taking the oath of citizenship so that authorities could verify that they had recited the oath.[19. See U.S. Department of State. July 28, 2014. "Canada." 2013 Report on International Religious Freedom.] In April 2013, a judge in the Canadian province of Ontario ruled that a Muslim woman had to remove her face-covering veil in order to testify in a sexual assault case. The Canadian Supreme Court had ruled in 2012 that presiding judges should make such decisions on a case-by-case basis.[14]

Regulation of religious dress is one of 20 items that make up Pew Research Center's annual index measuring the extent of government restrictions on religion around the world. To track this and other indicators of government restrictions on religion, researchers comb through more than a dozen publicly available, widely cited sources of information, including the U.S. State Department's annual reports on international religious freedom and annual reports from the U.S. Commission on International Religious Freedom, as well as reports from several independent, nongovernmental organizations and a variety of European and United Nations bodies.[21. For more details on the index and the sources, see the Methodology for Pew Research Center's February 2015 report "Latest Trends in Religious Restrictions and Hostilities."] If an incident is mentioned in one of these sources, researchers may search newspaper articles or other sources for additional details to flesh out the anecdotes used to illustrate the restrictions.

The Center's studies on religious restrictions are part of the Pew-Templeton Global Religious Futures project, which analyzes religious change and its impact on societies around the world. This project is jointly funded by The Pew Charitable Trusts and the John Templeton Foundation.

Women also faced harassment over religious dress

Even in countries that do not officially regulate women's attire, women sometimes face social pressure to conform to local customs or societal norms concerning religious dress. Failure to comply can lead to harassment or acts of hostility directed at women by private individuals, organizations or social groups. This includes cases in which women are harassed for wearing religious dress, as well as cases in which they are harassed for perceived violations of religious dress codes. Pew Research Center's latest study on religious restrictions and hostilities finds that more than 50 countries had at least one incident involving this type of harassment in 2013.[15]

Harassment of women over religious dress is one of the 13 measures that make up Pew Research Center's annual index measuring the extent of social hostilities involving religion across the world.[16] To track harassment of women over religious dress, researchers at the Center comb through the same information sources used to track government restrictions on religion.

It is important to note that the coding of this measure simply reflects the presence or absence of harassment in a particular country, not the extent of the harassment. A country that had a single incident of harassment is coded the same as one that had widespread harassment. It is also very likely that the sources do not capture every incident of harassment in a particular country, especially incidents that occurred within families. In addition, the definition of harassment used in the sources is very broad, covering everything from name-calling to physical assaults. The sources do not attempt to differentiate between the types of harassment or determine the severity of the harassment. However, the sources are particularly likely to take note of very serious incidents of harassment and high-profile incidents that result in media coverage. Therefore, the coding of this measure gives a general sense of how widespread such harassment is around the world and how it may contribute to the climate of human rights and religious freedom in particular countries.

As noted above, the question included in the Social Hostilities Index ("were women harassed for violating religious dress codes?") does not differentiate between harassment of women for wearing religious attire or for not wearing religious attire. For this report, researchers went back and recoded the data from 2012 and 2013 to determine how many countries had reports of each type of harassment.

During this two-year period, women were harassed for wearing religious dress in 33 of the 198 countries (17%). By contrast, women were harassed for not abiding by religious dress codes in 23 of the 198 countries (12%). There were relatively few countries in which both types of harassment occurred in 2012 and 2013 (five countries, or 3%).

In general, harassment of women over religious dress was in line with government laws, policies or regulations. For instance, in the 39 countries that restricted women's ability to wear certain kinds of religious attire, two-thirds of all incidents of harassment involved women who were wearing such attire. And in the 12 countries that mandated some form of religious dress, all the incidents of harassment reported in the study's sources involved women who failed to abide by the dress codes.

Type of harassment women faced over religious dress varied by region

When it comes to reported incidents of harassment, Europe stands out in one key respect: In nearly half of the region's countries (21 of 45), there was at least one report of women being harassed for wearing religious attire in 2012-2013. This is a higher percentage than in the four other regions included in the study.

Virtually all of the incidents in Europe reported in the study's sources involved Muslim women.[17] One of the cases involved a young Muslim woman in Spain who finished near the top of her university class in pharmacology but found it difficult to find a job because she did not want to remove her veil.[25. See Spitálszky, Andrea. 2013. "National Shadow Reports 2012-2013: Spain."

European Network Against Racism.] In France, two men attacked a pregnant Muslim woman in the Parisian suburb of Argenteuil on June 13, 2013, kicking her in the stomach and attempting to remove her headscarf and cut her hair; she subsequently suffered a miscarriage.[18]

Relatively few European countries (three of the 45, or 7%) had incidents in which women were harassed for not wearing religious attire. One country that did was Russia. Women in the Russian republic of Chechnya were pressured to wear headscarves in public places as part of President Ramzan Kadyrov's so-called "virtue campaign," and in the Chechen capital of Grozny, several women were attacked with paintball guns when they appeared in public without wearing headscarves.[19]

The Middle East and North Africa was the region that had the highest percentage of countries where women were harassed for not wearing religious dress. Eight of the region's 20 countries (40%) had such incidents in 2012 and 2013. In July 2012, for example, Islamist rebels occupying a neighborhood in Aleppo, Syria, issued a fatwa, or religious edict, requiring all Muslim women to abide by conservative standards of dress, including prohibitions on tight-fitting clothes and makeup.[20] In Tunisia, a female journalist reported being attacked in Tunis in May 2013 for wearing a sleeveless summer dress.[29. See Human Rights Watch. 2013. "Tunisia. World Report 2013."] Not all of the victims of this type of harassment were Muslims, however. In Israel, for instance, a group of ultra-Orthodox Jews (also known as Haredi Jews) assaulted a woman in Ramat Beit Shemesh in January 2012, smashing her car windows and hitting her in the head with a rock because they thought she was dressed immodestly.[30. See Rosenberg, Oz. Jan. 25, 2012. "Woman in Beit Shemesh Attacked by Ultra-Orthodox Extremists." Haaretz. For context, also see U.S. Department of State. July 28, 2014. "Israel." 2013 Report on International Religious Freedom.]

The Asia-Pacific region had roughly equal shares of countries where women were harassed for wearing religious dress and not wearing religious dress (14% in the first case, 16% in the latter).

Both types of harassment often involved Muslim women. For instance, a private Catholic college in the Philippines caused a controversy in August 2012 when it banned Muslim students from wearing headscarves, before reversing the policy under pressure from students and the local National Council on Muslim Filipinos. [31. See U.S. Department of State. May 20, 2013. "The Philippines." 2012 Report on International Religious Freedom. Also see Aug. 5, 2012. "Philippine School Bans Students from Wearing Hijab." Agence France-Presse.] In Malaysia, women reportedly faced strong social pressure to wear the Tudung, a local form of dress that involves a headscarf.[21]

Harassment of women over religious dress occurred in less than 15% of the 48 countries in sub-Saharan Africa in 2012 and 2013. Women were harassed for wearing religious dress in three countries in the region (6%) and for not wearing religious dress in four countries (8%). Women in southern Nigeria, for example, were said to have faced employment discrimination for wearing headscarves, particularly in positions requiring interactions with customers, such as those in the banking industry.[33. See U.S. Department of State May 20, 2013. "Nigeria." 2012 Report on International Religious Freedom.] And women in Mali who did not wear full-face veils were subjected to beatings, floggings and arbitrary arrest at the hands of al-Qaeda in the Islamic Maghreb, which occupied the northern part of the country throughout much of 2013.[22] In Swaziland – where nearly 90% of the population is Christian – women were told not to wear pants and miniskirts in some areas of the country, including areas under the jurisdiction of "traditional authorities" and around the residences of tribal leaders.[23]

In the Americas, there were reports of women being harassed for wearing religious dress in one of the region's 35 countries, Canada. After Quebec's ruling political party, Parti Québécois, introduced a controversial "charter of values" in 2013 that would have prohibited government employees from wearing "conspicuous" religious symbols, women's centers in the province reported an increase in verbal and physical attacks on Muslim women.[36.

See Human Rights Watch. 2014. "World Report 2014: Canada." Also see Peritz, Ingrid, and Les Perreaux. Sept. 10, 2013. "Quebec Reveals Religious Symbols to be Banned from Public Sector." The Globe and Mail. The proposed "charter of values" died the following year, after Parti Quebecois was defeated in Quebec's 2014 general election. See Séguin, Rhéal. April 7, 2014. "Marois to Step Down in Wake of Stunning Defeat at the Hands of Liberals." *The Globe and Mail.*] The sources used for this study cited no reports of women being harassed in the Americas for not wearing religious dress in 2012 and 2013.

There were no reports in the study's sources of women being harassed over religious dress in the United States in 2012-2013. However, it is important to note that the data collection process for the U.S. is slightly different than for the rest of the world since one of the primary sources used for the study – the U.S. State Department's International Religious Freedom Report – does not cover the U.S. To make sure events in the U.S. are not overlooked, researchers examine reports from the U.S. Department of Justice and the FBI, as well as those primary sources that do include data on the United States, including reports by the Anti-Defamation League, the United Nations, Human Rights Watch, the International Crisis Group and the United Kingdom Foreign & Commonwealth Office. Overall, the U.S. has moderate levels of both government restrictions on religion and social hostilities toward religious groups, ranking somewhere in the middle range of nearly 200 countries analyzed in Pew Research Center's most recent report on religious restrictions and hostilities worldwide.[24]

Endnotes

1. For more details, see Pew Research Center's February 2015 report "Latest Trends in Religious Restrictions and Hostilities."
2. See U.S. Department of State. July 28, 2014. "Russia." 2013 Report on International Religious Freedom. Also see Barry, Ellen. March 18, 2013. "Local Russian Hijab Ban Puts Muslims in a Squeeze." The New York Times.
3. For background, see Human Rights Watch. Dec. 21, 2010. "Questions and Answers on Restrictions on Religious Dress and Symbols in Europe."
4. See U.S. Department of State. July 28, 2014. "France." 2013 Report on International Religious Freedom. According to the State Department's 2012 Report on International

Religious Freedom: "The policy of the police is not to enforce the law in private locations, or around places of worship, where the law's application would unduly interfere with the free exercise of religion. ... If an individual refuses to remove the garment, police may take the person to the local police station to verify his or her identity. However, an individual may not be questioned or held for more than four hours." Also see Willsher, Kim. July 1, 2014. "France's Burqa Ban Upheld by Human Rights Court." The Guardian.

5. See U.S. Department of State. July 28, 2014. "Belgium." 2013 Country Reports on Human Rights Practices. Also see July 23, 2011. "Belgian Ban on Full Veils Comes Into Force." BBC News.

6. See U.S. Department of State. May 20, 2013. "Belgium." 2012 Report on International Religious Freedom. Also see Chaib, Saila Ouald. Dec. 14, 2012. "Belgian Constitutional Court says Ban on Face Coverings Does not Violate Human Rights." The Strasbourg Observer.

7. See U.S. Department of State. May 20, 2013. "Saudi Arabia." 2012 Report on International Religious Freedom. Also see S.B. Jan. 28, 2015. "Saudi Arabia's Dress Code for Women" The Economist.

8. See Human Rights Without Frontiers Newsletters. 2012. Egypt. Also see Nov. 11, 2012. "EgyptAir Stewardesses Begin Wearing Hijab." Agence France-Presse.

9. See U.S. Department of State. July 28, 2014. "Israel and the Occupied Territories – the Occupied Territories." 2013 Report on International Religious Freedom. Also see Badarni, Hadeel. July 2013. "From the Testimony of a Palestinian Woman Prisoner." The Public Committee Against Torture in Israel.

10. See U.S. Department of State May 20, 2013. "Oman." 2012 Report on International Religious Freedom.

11. See U.S. Department of State. May 20, 2013. "Iran." 2012 Report on International Religious Freedom. Also see Erdbrink, Thomas. Oct. 5, 2015. "Cautiously, Iranians Reclaim Public Spaces and Liberties Long Suppressed." The New York Times.

12. See U.S. Department of State. May 20, 2013. "Somalia." 2012 Report on International Religious Freedom. In 2013, Pew Research Center changed the way it coded government restrictions in Somalia. In 2012 and earlier years of the study, researchers coded actions by al-Shabaab as government restrictions, largely because the group effectively controlled large swathes of Somali territory. The extent of al-Shabaab control over Somali territory decreased in calendar year 2013, so researchers did not code their actions as government restrictions but rather as social hostilities. This contributed to a drop in Somalia's score on the Government Restrictions Index in 2013, even though actual practices by the government did not change appreciably.

13. See U.S. Department of State. July 28, 2014. "Mozambique." 2013 Report on International Religious Freedom; and Freedom House. 2013. "Mozambique." Freedom in the World 2013. Also see Aug. 9, 2011. "Muslims Protest Against the Veil Ban." The Economist Intelligence Unit.

14. See U.S. Department of State. July 28, 2014. "Canada." 2013 Report on International Religious Freedom.

15. See Pew Research Center's February 2015 report "Latest Trends in Religious Restrictions and Hostilities."

16. For more details on the index, see Pew Research Center's February 2015 report "Latest Trends in Religious Restrictions and Hostilities."

17. For a complete list of the sources, see Pew Research Center's February 2015 report "Latest Trends in Religious Restrictions and Hostilities." Pages 38-40.

18. See U.S. Department of State. July 28, 2014. "France." 2013 Report on International Religious Freedom. Also see Erlanger, Stephen. June 18, 2013. "Muslim Woman Suffers Miscarriage After Attack in France." New York Times.

19. See Human Rights Watch. 2013. "Russia. World Report 2013." Also see Human Rights Watch. 2012. "Virtue Campaign on Women in Chechnya Under Ramzan Kadyrov."

20. See U.S. Department of State. July 28, 2014. "Syria." 2013 Report on International Religious Freedom. Also see Solomon, Erika. July 1, 2013. "Islamists in Syria's Aleppo Ban 'Provocative Dress' for Syria's Women." Reuters.

21. See U.S. Department of State. July 28, 2014. "Malaysia." 2013 Report on International Religious Freedom.

22. See Human Rights Watch. 2014. "World Report 2014: Mali. Also see Nossiter, Adam. June 2, 2012. "In Timbuktu, Harsh Change Under Islamists." New York Times.

23. See U.S. Department of State. July 28, 2014. "Swaziland." 2013 Country Reports on Human Rights Practices. Also see Aug. 3, 2013. "Swazi Chief Bans Miniskirts and Trousers for Women." Agence France-Presse.

See Pew Research Center's February 2015 report "Latest Trends in Religious Restrictions and Hostilities." Also see Pew Research Center's March 25, 2015, Fact Tank post, "How the U.S. compares with the rest of the world on religious restrictions."

In France the "Burkini" Makes Muslim Women Feel Conflicted

Eleanor Beardsley

In the following viewpoint, Eleanor Beardsley argues that a new Islamic fashion is making women in France feel conflicted. Sold by British retailer Marks and Spencer, the "burkini," or a full-body swimsuit, is toeing the line of what is allowed or appropriate in France, especially considering the 2004 ban on the headscarf in French public schools and government offices. The author finishes with a quote from a French Muslim woman who describes being Muslim in France as "becoming more and more complicated." Beardsley is NPR's Paris correspondent.

As you read, consider the following questions:

1. What year was French secularism established?
2. In what major city does Marks and Spencer have stores in and around?
3. What is the name of at least one designer of "Islamic fashion" discussed in the beginning of the article?

S ome major designers are launching fashion lines aimed at Muslim women — loose-fitting tunics and skirts with accompanying head veils. Once destined for markets in the Middle

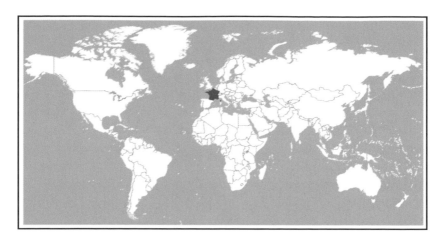

East, such clothing is gaining mainstream appeal in the West. In stores across Europe, "Islamic fashion" is now becoming available from top designers such as Dolce & Gabbana and DKNY.

But Paris shopper Nellie Bertrand says she feels conflicted by the trend, especially the women's bathing suit with trousers and a hood. It's dubbed the "burkini," now sold by the British retailer Marks and Spencer's, which has stores in and around Paris.

"Honestly, it's really complicated," Bertrand says. "Because, you know, people are supposed to be able to wear what they want. But in France, we're not used to having those kind of clothes in schools and they are not allowed."

Bertrand is referring to a 2004 ban on the Muslim headscarf in French public schools and government offices.

The debate over Islamic fashion turned into an uproar after Laurence Rossignol, the French women's rights minister, spoke about it in a radio interview in late March.

"We can't let these forces dictate what women wear," she said. When the interviewer pointed out that many women choose to wear the veil, Rossignol said, "Yeah, sure, like some American Negroes supported slavery."

With Europe's largest Muslim population, France is struggling to balance tolerance, secularism and personal freedom in a climate of heightened fear and security following two Islamist terrorist attacks in the last year. A state of emergency has been in place since November.

"Anytime you speak about Muslim women and anything dealing with Muslims in France, it becomes a hysterical debate," says Yasser Louati, who heads the French Collective Against Islamophobia.

Rossignol, he says, "is the minister for women's rights, and among those rights is the right to dress however you decide to dress."

Rossignol later said she regretted her remarks. But others in France have expressed similar misgivings. Feminist philosopher Elisabeth Badinter called for a boycott of brands selling Islamic fashion, and Paris Mayor Anne Hidalgo said she found the trend a little "upsetting."

Paris-based fashion writer Dana Thomas says fashion has long incorporated religious symbols. Take Dolce & Gabbana's embrace of Catholicism.

"They have pictures of nuns and priests in their ads and they have baroque crosses as jewelry and that's all OK," she says. "I think France is freaking out about this right now because they're just very nervous. And the French have always prided themselves on what they call laic, this system of separation of church and state, and so they have to react in this way in order to shore up the argument for the ant-veil law – that we just don't have anything religious creeping into our everyday lives."

French secularism was established by a 1905 law that strictly separated the church and state. At the time, the law aimed to keep a powerful Catholic church from dictating policy. While secularism is meant to ensure the state's neutrality with regard to religion and ensure that all religions can practice freely, many feel it is now being exhorted to discourage religion — especially Islam.

Faïza Zerouala is a French journalist and a Muslim. Her book, *Voices Behind the Veil*, tells the story of 10 French women who wear the hijab.

"To be Muslim in France is becoming more and more complicated," she says, "because we are talking so much about

Islam and its negative offshoots. And women who wear the veil are on the front line, because people can't help but somehow associate them with these attacks."

Zerouala says secularism is being used today as a shield against Islam. It's unacceptable to say you're anti-Muslim, she explains. But it's okay to say you're fighting to defend secularism.

Periodical and Internet Sources Bibliography

The following articles have been selected to supplement the diverse views presented in this chapter.

Antonia Blumberg, "Why These 6 Religious Groups Wear What They Wear," Huffington Post, August 18, 2015. https://www. huffingtonpost.com/entry/why-these-six-religious-groups-wear-what-they-wear_us_55ce7bcae4b055a6dab07ad0

Elizabeth Bucar, "How Muslim Women Use Fashion to Exert Political Influence," The Atlantic, February 1, 2018. https://www. theatlantic.com/international/archive/2018/02/muslim-women-fashion-political-influence/550256/

Angel Krasimirov, "Bulgaria bans full-face veils in public places," Reuters, Sept. 30, 2016, https://www.reuters.com/article/us-religion-burqa-bulgaria/bulgaria-bans-full-face-veils-in-public-places-idUSKCN1201FV.

Asra Q. Nomani and Hala Arafa, "As Muslim women, we actually ask you not to wear the hijab in the name of interfaith solidarity," The Washington Post, Dec. 21, 2015, https://www.washingtonpost. com/news/acts-of-faith/wp/2015/12/21/as-muslim-women-we-actually-ask-you-not-to-wear-the-hijab-in-the-name-of-interfaith-solidarity/?utm_term=.bdc13651077e.

Madison Park, "Quebec bars people with face coverings from getting public services," CNN, Oct. 19, 2017, https://www.cnn. com/2017/10/19/americas/quebec-face-covering-bill/index.html.

Janet Street-Porter, "An employer who bans all religious clothing at work is not one I'd want to work for," Independent, Mar. 17, 2017, http://www.independent.co.uk/voices/hijab-headscarf-ban-employment-law-not-one-id-want-to-work-for-a7636061.html.

Michaël Privot, "Ban on headscarves and religious clothing is discrimination," Euractiv Network, Jul. 15, 2016, https://www. euractiv.com/section/social-europe-jobs/opinion/ban-on-headscarves-and-religious-clothing-is-discrimination/.

Yair Rosenberg, "Global Plus: Religious Attire in the Public Square," International Association of Religion Journalists, September 16, 2015. https://www.theiarj.org/blog/2015/09/16/global-plus-religious-attire-in-the-public-square/

GLOBALVIEWPOINTS

CHAPTER 3

Religious Clothing and Public Schools

In the United States Teachers Must Be Aware of How Much They Disclose to Students

Marisa Fasciano

In the following viewpoint, Marisa Fasciano discusses just how much teachers can disclose about their personal religious beliefs to students in public schools. Teachers have a duty to encourage religious understanding but also must be objective when it comes to speaking about religion in the classroom, the author argues. Additionally, there are guidelines that some teachers must follow when it comes to their religious attire or jewelry so as to not make it stand out too much to their students. Fasciano is an Education Program Associate at the Tanenbaum Center for Interreligious Understanding.

As you read, consider the following questions:

1. Are public school teachers allowed to engage in personal prayer while in the presence of students?
2. What Act of 1964 requires employers, including schools, to reasonably accommodate the religious practices of an employee, unless doing so would create an undue hardship on the employer?
3. What is described as "unobtrusive" jewelry?

"Can I Say That? Can I Wear That?" by Marisa Fasciano, Southern Poverty Law Center, June 16, 2014. Reprinted with permission from Teaching Tolerance. www.tolerance.org.

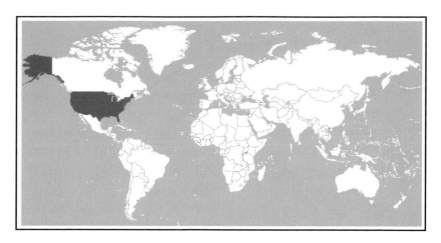

How much can teachers disclose about their personal religious and nonreligious beliefs to students? What should they do if, for example, a student asks about a religious symbol that they're wearing? To find answers to the question "Can I say or wear that?" a useful starting point is to see what the law permits and what it does not.

Title VII of the Civil Rights Act of 1964 requires employers, including schools, to reasonably accommodate the religious practices of an employee, unless doing so would create an undue hardship on the employer. Yet public schools must also comply with the U.S. Constitution's Establishment Clause, which prevents employees from advocating a particular belief system in front of students. These two legal forces can, at times, come into conflict and create ambiguity and uncertainty for school personnel.

In their capacity as government representatives, public school teachers should strike a balance between exercising their First Amendment rights to freedom of speech and religion and maintaining religious neutrality in the classroom. Independent school teachers, as well as parochial school teachers whose faith differs from that of their school, must also be mindful of the fine line between sharing their religious identity and promoting their belief system.

May public school teachers discuss their religious identity and views with students?

What do you say when a student asks, "Do you believe in God?" or "What religion do you practice?" Coming up with an appropriate response can be a challenge. Teachers have a responsibility to encourage religious understanding and to avoid the impression that religion is a taboo subject. They also have a right to talk about their religious identity and views when directly asked by students, or within the context of class discussion; however, they need to do so in an objective manner that specifies the personal nature of their experiences and perspective.

A student's age should be taken into account when formulating a response, especially because younger children are more likely to feel pressured into adopting an authority figure's viewpoint. Also, they may be less inclined to distinguish a teacher's identity from the school's identity. It's best to make absolutely clear that the student is in no way being taught to believe similarly or to conform to certain religious practices. Phrases such as "I believe that … " or "In my tradition … " help avoid the appearance of proselytizing.

May public school teachers wear religious clothing or jewelry to school?

Teachers can wear clothing or jewelry symbolizing their religious beliefs as long as the clothing or jewelry is not proselytizing or disruptive. However, the courts have often disagreed on the definitions of "proselytizing" and "disruptive" and ruled inconsistently on this issue. Some courts have weighted a teacher's right to free expression more heavily than the Establishment Clause does, and others have done the reverse.

The First Amendment Center claims that case law usually permits "unobtrusive" jewelry, such as a cross or Star of David necklace, but not a T-shirt with a proselytizing message. For example, in *Downing v. West Haven Board of Education* (2001), a federal district court ruled in favor of high school administrators who had ordered a teacher to remove or cover up a T-shirt that

Can a Teacher Wear Religious Garb to School?

Probably not. It is likely that many courts would allow a school to prohibit teachers' religious garb in order to maintain religious neutrality.

Pennsylvania and Oregon have laws that prohibit teachers from wearing religious clothing to schools. Both laws have been upheld in court challenges brought under the First Amendment and Title VII, the major anti-discrimination employment law. The courts reasoned that the statutes furthered the states' goal of ensuring neutrality with respect to religion in the schools.

In the Pennsylvania case, *U.S. v. Board of Education*, the 3rd Circuit rejected the Title VII religious-discrimination claim of a Muslim teacher who was prevented from wearing her religious clothing to school. The school acted pursuant to a state law, called the "Garb Statute," which provided: "[N]o teacher in any public school shall wear in said school or while engaged in the performance of his duty as such teacher any dress, mark, emblem or insignia indicating the fact that such teacher is a member or adherent of any religious order, sect or denomination."

The teacher and the Equal Employment Opportunity Commission contended that the school should have allowed the teacher to wear her head scarf and long, loose dress as a "reasonable accommodation" of her religious faith. The appeals court disagreed, determining that "the preservation of religious neutrality is a compelling state interest."

In its 1986 decision *Cooper v. Eugene School District*, the Oregon Supreme Court rejected the free-exercise challenge of a Sikh teacher suspended for wearing religious clothing—a white turban and white clothes—to her special education classes. The Oregon high court upheld the state law, which provided: "No teacher in any public school shall wear any religious dress while engaged in the performance of duties as a teacher." The court wrote that "the aim of maintaining the religious neutrality of the public schools furthers a constitutional obligation beyond an ordinary policy preference of the legislature."

The First Amendment Center's A Teacher's Guide to Religion in the Public Schools provides that "teachers are permitted to wear non-obtrusive jewelry, such as a cross or Star of David. But teachers should not wear clothing with a proselytizing message (e.g. a 'Jesus Saves' T-shirt)."

"Can a teacher wear religious garb to school, provided the teacher does not proselytize to the students?" Newseum Institute.

read "JESUS 2000 — J2K." The court argued that this teacher's First Amendment rights must give way to the school's Establishment Clause concerns. In other words, the teacher could not appear to be promoting a religion.

Even religious garb without a proselytizing message has been perceived by the courts as endorsing a particular faith. Federal courts have upheld laws in Pennsylvania and Oregon that prohibit teachers from wearing religious garb. In the Pennsylvania case, *U.S. v. Board of Education* (1990), a Muslim teacher and the Equal Employment Opportunity Commission had filed a Title VII religious discrimination suit because the teacher could not wear her headscarf (hijab) and long, loose dress to school. They argued that allowing such dress was a "reasonable accommodation," but the court claimed that the state had a "compelling state interest" to preserve religious neutrality.

This case illustrates the subjectivity of the definition of religious neutrality and raises some difficult questions. Does wearing religious garb, like a hijab, detract from the religious neutrality of the classroom? How does prejudice and stereotyping influence legal decisions about religious neutrality? Are all religions treated equally?

May public school teachers pray in school?

As stated by the U.S. Department of Education, "When acting in their official capacities as representatives of the state, teachers, school administrators, and other school employees are prohibited by the Establishment Clause from encouraging or discouraging prayer, and from actively participating in such activity with students." In addition, they cannot engage in personal prayer while in the presence of students because students may perceive such activity as promoting religion.

On the other hand, when it's clear that school employees are acting individually, such as during a lunch break or in a faith-based group that meets before or after school hours, they are within their rights to pray or otherwise express their religious beliefs.

Helpful Tips

So where do these laws and guidelines leave us? Given the complexity of the issue, teachers may find it helpful to consult fellow educators and their administration for guidance as they balance staying true to their belief systems (religious or nonreligious) in the classroom with following the law. Moving forward, you might find it helpful to keep in mind these simple tips:

- Ask your school administration to provide clear guidelines about religious expression if they are not already well articulated.

- Think ahead about what your students are already curious about and have a few prepared responses in mind.

- Use "I" statements to be sure that students don't misinterpret your personal views as representing the school or an entire religious group.

- Be mindful of students' ages because younger students tend to be more impressionable.

- Put yourself in a parent's shoes when considering how to share your religious identity and views with children.

Opt out respectfully if you don't feel comfortable answering a question for any reason. You can simply say, "Thank you for asking me, but I'd rather not discuss it."

Keep in mind your rights, as well as the legal responsibilities of educators, as you consider the place of your belief system in the classroom.

Secularism May Oppress People Seeking Religious Freedom

Rahul Mohanty

In the following excerpted viewpoint, Rahul Mohanty argues that the rules and regulations of religious attire and symbols within public schools around the globe vary widely. For example, France is strict in terms of keeping religious symbols or clothing in public under wraps, while Switzerland is a lot more lenient and even promotes a co-op model between religion and public education. Overall, the majority of countries do their best to keep public education and religion separate. Mohanty is a lawyer based in India.

As you read, consider the following questions:

1. What year did the French parliament pass a law prohibiting the concealment of one's face in public?
2. What university was involved in *Sahin v. Turkey*?
3. In South Africa, a rastafarian student was suspended for five days from school for doing what?

In this paper I will be examining the Secular State's approach towards religious symbols in public schools in a comparative constitutional method. Here in religious symbols I have included the symbols and other religious clothing and attires worn by members of several religions.

"Religious symbols and attire in public schools: A comparative constitutional analysis," by Rahul Mohanty, Manupatra Information Solutions Pvt. Ltd., January 2014. Reprinted by permission.

In light of the current controversies regarding right to display religious symbols in schools, colleges and other public institutions it has become necessary to do a comparative analysis of several multicultural and 'secular' societies and draw some lessons from them. Although secular values and privacy of religion is being increasingly accepted, there is a danger that secularism itself may degenerate into a dogma and may become oppressive for people by violating their freedom of religion. This paper is therefore an attempt in this direction of finding a pragmatic solution to this problem.

This issue has created a storm of controversies especially in Europe. There are several facets of this controversy. First pertains to display of religious symbols in schools and display of religious symbols by the teachers.

France

France guarantees equality of all irrespective of religion.[1] However the strict separation between religion and state practised in France is well known. France embodies the enlightenment principle of religion is private matter and it should not be brought into "public sphere" in its fullest extent. It follows the doctrine of *laïcité* i.e. the neutrality of the state towards religious beliefs, and the complete isolation of religious and public spheres which translates into the French state and government not taking a position on any religion or its practices.[2] However, in practical terms it means the separation between a person's private and public life must be complete. He/she has to practise his/her religion in private sphere only and should not bring it to public sphere and thus it should not affect everyday life of the person.[3] Thus, nothing connected to religion is allowed to appear in public life of a person.[4]

However, the major problem with this approach is most religions are not compatible with staying private. More often than not, the religious codes strive to regulate entire life of a person and do not differentiate between public and private lives. Thus, if a religion prescribes certain attire, it has to be worn always irrespective of private and public life. The French government had enacted a law in 2004 banning 'conspicuous religious symbols' such as Muslim headscarf, Sikh turbans, Jewish skullcap and large Christian crucifixes in schools.[5] In 2010 the French parliament passed a law prohibiting the concealment of one's face in public which prevents Muslim veils that cover the face in all public places and not only in schools.[6] This law, approved by the French Constitutional Council, makes it a crime to coerce women to wear such veils.[7] This had created huge debates and protests by minorities especially from Muslims who saw it as directed against Islamic Headscarf which Muslim women were obligated to wear.[8] However, the French government did not back out but justified the move on basis of its 'deep secular roots' and *laïcité* principle.[9] This position is completely different from that of the principles followed by South Africa, India etc. Even most other countries of Europe have only declined to interfere when the school or local administration has imposed such a ban or their judiciary has effectively banned them but few countries indeed have actively banned religious attires in schools.

Switzerland

The 1999 constitution of Switzerland provides in its general equality clause that *"No person may be discriminated against, in particular on grounds of origin, race, gender, age, language, social position, way of life, religious, ideological, or political convictions, or because of a physical, mental or psychological disability."*[10] Article 15 which pertains to freedom of religion and conscience guarantees freedom of religion and conscience, gives people right to practice and profess any religion they want and says that each person has right to join any religious organisation but they may not be forced to do so.[11] Article 72 makes Cantons (provinces) responsible for relation between state and church and to preserve public peace among several communities.[12] The interesting observation about The Swiss constitution does not expressly declare it to be secular, nor does it establish a state religion or church. However from the general equality clauses and freedom of religion clauses the proper inference would be that it establishes a secular state.

Coming to the judicial interpretations regarding secularity, doctrine of state impartiality and religious symbols in public schools has been considered in many cases. In the Swimming lessons case the Swiss Supreme Court allowed a Muslim father *"to remove his daughter from co-ed swimming lessons in the second year of primary school"* based on the Koranic dictum that females should cover their body from sexual maturity onwards.[13] Although in this case the girl was not sexually mature, nevertheless the court allowed the appeal on ground of 'strong faith'.[14] Although this case is not about religious symbols, it shows that the Swiss Courts were ready to consider religious beliefs of parents in deciding upon such cases. In the *Genevan vetements religieux* decision, the court held that although *"the scope of religious profession generally covers the right to wear religious clothing"* but on balance of reasonableness it was likely that the feeling of students and their parents will be hurt if a teacher wears such religious clothes and the aim of state should not only be espousing religious freedom but also achieving religious harmony.[15] It said the school might become a place of confrontation if teachers were allowed to wear religious clothes.[16] However, students have been generally allowed to wear religious attire.[17]

In the landmark *crocifisso* decision Swiss Federal Court ruled about the religious symbols in primary schools and upheld a cantonal council of Geneva a female primary school teacher's wearing an Islamic headscarf[18] and also decided on question that whether crucifixes attached to walls of every classroom violated the doctrine of state impartiality.[19] It held that it was important to observe religious and denominational impartiality in public schools as the education was compulsory and children from many religions studied there. Thus, display of religious symbols like crucifixes in classrooms could conceivably be seen as instruction to follow Christian precepts in education and offend people and make an impression on young students.

However, it is has been said that children wearing religious attire like headscarves would be allowed in Switzerland.[20]

Endnotes

1 1946 CONST. 1946.

2 Frederick Mark Gedicks, Religious Exemptions, Formal Neutrality, and Laïcité, Indiana Journal of Global Legal Studies , Volume 13, Issue 2, Summer 2006 pp. 473-492 10.1353/gls.2006.0014; The concept of Laïcité in France, http://www.normandyvision. org/ article12030701.php (Last visited on: 21-07-2013).

3 *Ibid.*

4 *Id.*

5 French scarf ban comes into force, http://news.bbc.co.uk/2/hi/3619988.stm (last accessed

on: 21-07-2013).

6 Questions and Answers on Restrictions on Religious Dress and Symbols in Europe, http://www.hrw.org/news/2010/12/21/questions-and-answers-restrictions-religious-dress- and-symbols-europe (Last visited on: 21-07-2013).

7 *Ibid.* 8 *Id.*

9 *Id.*

10 Constitution fédérale de la Confédération Suisse [Cst] [Constitution] April 18, 1999 art. 8.

11 Constitution fédérale de la Confédération Suisse [Cst] [Constitution] April 18, 1999 art. 15.

12 Constitution fédérale de la Confédération Suisse [Cst] [Constitution] April 18, 1999 art. 72.

13 Cavelti, U. J., "Die Religionsfreiheit in Sonderstatusverhältnissen," Pahud de Mortanges, R. (ed.), Religiöse Minderheiten und Recht, Freiburg i. Ue. 1998 (Freiburger Veröffentlichungen zum Religionsrecht, volume 1), 51; Angehrn, M., Volksschulen und lokale Schulbehörden vor neuen Herausforderungen, dissertation St. Gallen 2004, 162 ff.

14 *Ibid.*

15 *Id.*

16 Marcel Stiissi, Religious Symbols in Switzerland.

17 BGE 116 Ia 252, E. 7, S. 262 f.

18 Code of practice of the Swiss Supreme Court 47 (1998), 295.

19 *Ibid.*

20 Stiissi, op.cit., supra. C.f. Gloor (ann. 21), 2; Jean Francois Aubert, L'islam a l'ecole publique, Ehrenzeller, B. u.a. (ed.), Festschrift ffir Yvo Hangartener (Dike Verlag, St. Gallen 1998), 479 et seq.

In Turkey Headscarves Lead to Issues in Public Schools

Fariba Nawa

In the following viewpoint, Fariba Nawa argues that women in Turkey are still being judged in what is considered a conservative society, despite the government's lifting of the ban on headscarves in 2011. The author writes of two women who faced discrimination in Turkey because of their religion and choice to wear Muslim headscarves. One woman recounts having to take off her headscarf to participate in the debate team in high school and was even rejected from a public university in Istanbul because of her religious attire. Nawa is a journalist whose work has appeared in The Atlantic, Foreign Affairs, *and* Mother Jones, *among many other publications.*

As you read, consider the following questions:

1. How many people were surveyed across Turkey by a private consulting firm?
2. What year did Turkey's secular government originally ban the headscarf for civil servants and public universities?
3. What university did Betül choose where no one monitored her clothing?

In a café at Istanbul Arel University, a group of friends—secular and religious, Kurdish and Turkish—gather to talk about their

"Turkey's fraught history with headscarves," by Fariba Nawa, Public Radio International's The World, December 20, 2016. Reprinted by permission.

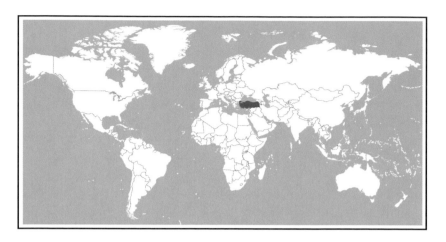

country's changing identity. One topic of discussion among two of the young women, Betül and Melis, is the headscarf.

Both women asked that we not use their last names to protect their privacy in Turkey's current political climate.

Betül, 21, began wearing a Muslim headscarf in 2011, just after it became legal in public universities and government institutions. But Betül says women in headscarves still faced discrimination. In high school she says she had to take off her headscarf when she participated in the debate team. And when she applied to the public Istanbul University, she was rejected. "I wanted to go to that university because my cousin was there, but they wouldn't admit me," she says.

She thinks it's because she wears a headscarf.

So Betül, who studies psychology, chose Arel, a private liberal university, where she says no one monitored her clothing.

Turkey's secular government outlawed the headscarf for civil servants and public universities in 1980, citing the need for the separation of state and religion. Religious women sometimes resisted, risking their jobs and degrees. They wore hats and wigs to go to school and work.

In 2011, Turkey's Islamist government lifted the ban. And in the past five years, secular Turkish women say they find themselves judged by an increasingly conservative society.

"It used to be that women in headscarves were mistreated, but now it's the opposite," Betül says. "We should have empathy for one another."

In a recent survey of 16,000 people across Turkey conducted by the private consulting firm Ipsos KMG, 60 percent of women said they wear a headscarf, and nearly half of the men said their wife should wear a headscarf.

Melis, who considers herself secular, also studies psychology. She says she's angry and frustrated by the negative attitudes about secular women she now encounters in Turkey. It's a real problem on public transportation, she says. She remembers one recent incident on a crowded metro, when there were no seats. "I was feeling sick and looking pale. A man kept staring at me," Melis says. "He didn't give me his seat but as soon as a covered girl around my age walked in, he offered his seat to her. He looked straight at me, but said to her: 'You deserve this seat.' I felt worthless."

Melis says she's thinking of leaving Turkey after she's done with her studies, maybe to travel to Europe. She doesn't feel like she fits in any more. "As someone who values my freedoms, I don't think the government protects my rights, and I don't think it will protect the rights of a child that I would raise. I believe [Turkey will] become much more conservative. That's why I don't want to stay here," Melis says.

The secular-Islamist polarization in Turkey plays out on women's bodies in public spaces. Those who cover are considered supporters of the ruling Justice and Development party, or AKP, and women who don't cover are seen as symbols of Turkey's secular tradition. The reality is more complicated than that. But the headscarf has been a contested symbol of liberation or oppression throughout modern Turkish history.

Nurbanu Dursun, a graduate student at the premier Bogazici University, says women in headscarves are accepted in public universities as students but not necessarily in academic positions. Dursun, who covers her head, says Turkey's intelligentsia is still dominated by secular women.

And in a few liberal neighborhoods of Istanbul, women in headscarves continue to be ridiculed as backward.

But in many conservative neighborhoods, women who don't cover face harassment. And it's not just dirty looks and name-calling. In September, during the Eid holiday, a man on a bus attacked a nurse, cutting her face. He shouted "women who wear shorts must die."

A protest broke out immediately after the attack was publicized. Women say if they don't raise their voices, the government pays little attention.

Human rights activists blame the AKP and President Recep Tayyip Erdogan's rhetoric of creating a "good woman, bad woman narrative" in Turkish life.

Erdogan has publicly encouraged women to be religious, marry, have at least three children and work only part-time. He has criticized secular, educated, single women without kids as "half women."

Emma Sinclair Webb, director of Human Rights Watch in Turkey, says the government can have a family values agenda, but it shouldn't discriminate against those who don't fit that mold. "These have been very insulting and polarizing discourses coming from above about women's roles and women's identity in this society," says Sinclair-Webb.

Betül and Melis, the two friends at Arel, say their government needs to be more pluralistic. Betül says she feels more at home in Turkey than Melis, but doesn't want to see women like Melis marginalized. They both say meeting each other has challenged their preconceptions. "I was a person with a lot of prejudice," says Melis. "I overcame this with Betül. Some of my opinions, particularly about women with headscarves, have changed."

As for Betül, she says one reason she chose this private university was to be among students who think differently from her. That's the best way to foster tolerance, she says, and she'll fight for respect for every woman, not just those wearing headscarves like her.

In France the Banning of Headscarves Leads to Religious and Social Unrest

Facing History and Ourselves

In the following viewpoint, Facing History and Ourselves argues that the banning of headscarves in France has caused religious and social unrest. The article explores various viewpoints from different women, with some groups believing that Muslim girls should keep their religious traditions to themselves, while others felt more open on the subject, questioning the secularity of schools, pointing out the fact that the majority of holidays on the school calendar revolve around the Catholic calendar. Facing History and Ourselves is a nonprofit organization that engages students in the examination of racism and prejudice.

As you read, consider the following questions:

1. What is assimilation?
2. Nearly what percent of the nation felt that the veil was an obstacle to France's national unity, to its secular and democratic tradition, and to its security?
3. Women who opposed the wearing of the headscarf felt that the veil promoted what?

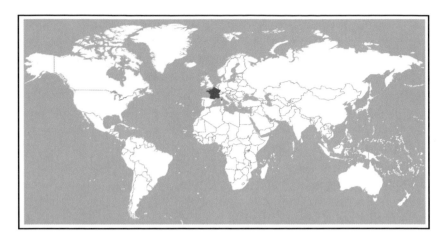

F rench citizens found themselves grappling with a number of pressing issues at the beginning of the new millennium. In predominantly French-Maghrebian neighborhoods, social unrest relating to poverty and discrimination was on the rise, compounding ethnic conflicts stemming from the real and imaginary differences between these North African French and the European French. Meanwhile, religious tensions surrounding the presence of a large Muslim population in a secular state flared, intensified by growing fears of Islamic radicalism following 9/11 and other terrorist attacks in Europe.

These tensions were especially sharp in public schools that had large numbers of Muslim students, and they soon seemed to focus on the Islamic veil. In 2004, roughly 70 percent of the nation felt that the veil was an obstacle to France's national unity, to its secular and democratic tradition, and to its security. Both Left and Right agreed: the veil had to be banned in public schools.

The year before, President Jacques Chirac had called on Bernard Stasi, a former minister, to head a commission to study the veil and other aspects of Muslim life that affected France's secular tradition. Lawmakers, school administrators, and the general public expected drastic actions.

However, little attention was paid to the question of why Muslim girls and women were wearing the veil. Sociologist Caitlin

Killian attempted to answer this question. During the debate, she interviewed female Muslim immigrants about a range of related issues including racism, assimilation, school curriculums, and teachers' attitudes toward the veil (or, in the case of men, the beards some Muslims wear).

The findings pointed to a broad spectrum of opinions regarding all of these issues. Focusing on the veil, Killian found, on the one hand, women who vigorously defended its ban in schools and, on the other, women who thought that the veil was a legitimate form of self-expression.

Some of the women Killian interviewed argued that there are much more urgent issues at school than the wearing of the veil (violence and poor behavior among them). According to others, the French are specifically targeting Muslim culture. They also thought that the proposed ban on headscarves in schools is driven by prejudice.

Yusra, a 31-year-old Moroccan, explained:

> I find that it's really an attitude on the part of teachers that is really racist, truly. That, for me, is a racist act. We cannot exclude girls because they wear the headscarf....It's really pointing a finger at them, and then [at] the culture of the child, they say to her "your culture, it's not good." You don't have a right to judge like that.

While some of the interviewees viewed the French reaction to the headscarf affair as racist, others questioned the of schools where most of the holidays and vacations revolved around the Catholic calendar. Some went on to suggest that instead of ignoring or banning Islamic traditions, teachers could use them to educate about the cultural and religious diversity of France's students.

Below are a few women's reflections:

> Besma, a 34-year-old Tunisian: I'm going to repeat what a lot of Arabs say, there are schools in France, or universities in France, where there are no exams on Saturday because it's the [Jewish] Sabbath, in the public schools, in the secular schools, and nobody talks about it. All that it takes is for the universities to agree....The students manage to make an [informal] arrangement with the

teachers....On Friday, they eat a lean meal, meaning a meatless meal because Catholics don't eat meat on Friday. We do Lent Friday in school cafeterias and nobody protests. Nobody finds anything to say. So I find it completely petty to hide behind arguments that don't hold up, that aren't at all convincing, and all of sudden there are different rules for different groups.

Nour, a 34-year-old Algerian: [Y]ou know the secular school, it doesn't miss celebrating Easter, and when they celebrate Easter, it doesn't bother me. My daughter comes home with painted Easter eggs and everything; it's pretty; it's cute. There are classes that are over 80 percent Maghrebian in the suburbs, and they celebrate Easter, they celebrate Christmas, you see? And that's not a problem for the secular school. And I don't find that fair....

I find that when it's Ramadan, they should talk about Ramadan. Honestly, me, it wouldn't be a problem. On the contrary, someone who comes into class...with a veil, that would pose a question actually, that we could discuss in class, to know why this person wears the veil....Why is it so upsetting to have someone in class who wears a veil, when we could make it a subject of discussion on all religions? Getting stuck on the veil hides the question. They make such a big deal out of it, the poor girls, they take them out of school; people turn them into extraterrestrials. In the end we turn them into people who will have problems in their identities, in their culture and everything....For a country that is home to so many cultures, there's no excuse.

Some of the women Killian interviewed argued that the veil is a symbol of a new identity, especially for the second-generation immigrants who experience rejection in their daily life in France. The veil, they suggested, is the response of those who seek alternatives to the French national identity. Isma, a 36-year-old Algerian teacher who now teaches in France, had this to say:

The girls who veil in France, especially the high school and junior high students, it's first of all a question of identity, because these girls are born in France to foreign parents....At a given time an adolescent wants to affirm himself, to show that he's someone, that he's an individual, so he thinks, I'd say, he thinks that it's by his clothes that he shows that he comes from somewhere [else], that he's someone [different]. So then, I think you should let them do it, and afterwards, by themselves, people come back to who they really are.

But other female immigrants argued that Muslims girls should assimilate or keep their traditions to themselves. Some felt that the veil promotes fundamentalism and intolerance, while others still saw it as a sign of female oppression:

Cherifa, a 44-year-old Moroccan: I believe that if they have to wear the veil then they should do it at home. Me, I'd be a bit radical. I wouldn't make concessions, because if I want to wear a djellaba [Middle Eastern cloak]...then I should stay in my country. I feel that when you are somewhere, you try to blend in. There's an old Moroccan proverb that says "do as your neighbor [does] or leave." That means that I shouldn't come to France to affirm my convictions, be they cultural or religious and all. If I want to wear babouches and put on the veil... well I should stay in my country, or I blend in. Otherwise, if I'm in France, well I'm sorry, I dress like the French. If I eat with them, live with them, if I go to their schools, I don't see why I'd make myself be noticed because I want to wear, um, they should wear it when they're at home or at friends. I don't have anything against it. But when she's at school and everything, I don't think so....No, I would totally agree with them outlawing the veil.

Deha, a 34-year-old Algerian: I come from a school [in Algeria] where the veil was already starting. It's not the way she dresses; it's what she is herself. The way she dresses implies a lot of things; so there are no sports, philosophy is forbidden....A girl who wears the veil [thinks that] she's pure and that the other who doesn't wear the veil, she's not pure. It's not that she's not pure; it's that she's a slut. You see? And it's there that you say to yourself, well, okay, the veil represents all of that.

Isma, a 36-year-old Algerian: I'm not intolerant; myself, I've suffered from intolerance, but dressing like that, you become yourself intolerant, because you want to impose. I'm sorry to say it, but it's often the one who wants to show that he's more Muslim than the other; he wants to impose it.

Periodical and Internet Sources Bibliography

The following articles have been selected to supplement the diverse views presented in this chapter.

Associated Press, "Nebraska Ends Ban on Religious Garb in Public Schools," Chicago Tribune, March 27, 2017. http://www.chicagotribune.com/news/nationworld/ct-nebraska-ban-religious-garb-20170327-story.html

Jessica Bakeman, "Senate votes 23-13 to protect religious expression in public schools," Politico, March 23, 2017, https://www.politico.com/states/florida/story/2017/03/senate-votes-23-13-to-protect-religious-expression-in-public-schools-110642.

David French, "Lawless Judges Have Created an America Where Praying Gets a Man Suspended from His Job," National Review, October 29, 2015. https://www.nationalreview.com/2015/10/praying-football-coach-religious-liberty-judicial-censorshp/

Benjamin Justice and Colin MacLeod, "Does Religion Have a Place in Public Schools?" The Atlantic, February 9, 2017. https://www.theatlantic.com/education/archive/2017/02/does-religion-have-a-place-in-public-schools/516189/

Kristina Rizga, "The Chilling Rise of Islamophobia in Our Schools," Mother Jones, January 26, 2016. https://www.motherjones.com/politics/2016/01/bullying-islamophobia-in-american-schools/

Todd Starnes, "School orders teachers to remove 'religious' items from classrooms," Fox News, October 4, 2016, http://www.foxnews.com/opinion/2016/10/04/school-orders-teachers-to-remove-religious-items-from-classrooms.html.

Deborah Strange, "Proposed law intended to protect religious expression in public schools," The Gainesville Sun, February 18, 2017, http://www.gainesville.com/news/20170218/proposed-law-intended-to-protect-religious-expression-in-public-schools.

Linda K. Wertheimer, "Teachers Can't Be Preachers," U.S. News, February 2, 2015, https://www.usnews.com/opinion/blogs/faith-matters/2015/02/02/jesus-sign-is-a-no-go-in-public-school-classroom.

CHAPTER 4

Dealing with Religious Clothing in Public Spaces

Religious Freedom and Women's Rights Go Hand in Hand

Thomas Reese

In the following viewpoint, Thomas Reese argues that the relationship between women's rights and religious freedom go hand in hand and support each other. The author writes that in some Middle Eastern countries, women are forced to dress a certain way due to religious traditions even if they are not in support of that tradition, and the fact that men can dictate what women wear is a violation of religious freedom and women's rights. Reese is a Jesuit priest and a senior analyst for National Catholic Reporter.

As you read, consider the following questions:

1. What commission is Thomas Reese the chair of?
2. What does religious freedom protect?
3. Religious freedom in its true meaning empowers women to do what?

S upport for religious freedom often appears to be in conflict with women's rights both in the United States and abroad. In the debate over the contraceptive mandate, for example, the religious freedom rights of employers were set against the right of their women employees. This conflict is real and will eventually be worked out in society and the courts.

But the conflict between religious freedom and women's rights is bad for both sides. If those supporting religious freedom are perceived as opposing women's rights, they will suffer because they are fighting against an historical force that is only going to get stronger. If those supporting women's rights are seen as against religious freedom, they will suffer because religion is so fundamental to most of the world's outlook on life.

This is a lose, lose situation.

But is conflict between religious freedom and women's rights inevitable? I would argue that it is not and that there are areas where women's rights and religious freedom go hand in hand and can support each other. Rather than opposing each other all the time, supporters of religious freedom and women's rights could work together on some issues.

I think that this is especially true in the area of international religious freedom — religious freedom outside the United States.

Although I am chair of the U.S. Commission on International Religious Freedom, what I write here does not necessarily represent the views of the commission.

It is true that there are legal and cultural practices supported by religious beliefs that treat women unequally in families, education, the workplace, and society. Examples would be female genital mutilation, forced marriages, honor killings, rigid dress codes, divorce laws favoring the husband, inheritance laws favoring male heirs, and restrictions on education, employment, and participation in political life.

Looked at one way, it appears that allowing freedom of religion is holding women down in these examples.

A way out of this apparent conflict is to emphasize that religious freedom is a human right that resides in the individual not in a religious tradition. "The human right to freedom of religion or belief does not protect religious traditions per se," explained Heiner Bielefeldt, the UN special rapporteur on freedom of religion or belief, "but instead facilitates the free search and development of faith-related identities of human beings, as individuals and in community with others."

Religious freedom does not protect religious belief or religious institutions from challenge. Rather religious freedom protects the right of an individual to believe or not believe, to change one's religion if one desires, and to speak and act on those beliefs. It protects believers not beliefs. Religious freedom includes freedom of speech and press on religious topics, which allows individuals to challenge religious beliefs and traditions.

As a result, religious freedom in its true meaning empowers women to decide for themselves what they will believe and empowers them to challenge the teachings of their own religion if they don't like the way it treats women. Any restrictions on the right of women to challenge religious beliefs and practices are violations of their religious freedom. With this kind of religious freedom the religious establishment can be challenged. Ultimately, it allows religions to evolve and change over time.

"In virtually all traditions," notes Bielefeldt, "one can indeed find persons or groups who make use of their freedom of religion or belief as a positive resource for the promotion of equality between men and women." When religious freedom is promoted, the position of these people is strengthened.

The fight over religious dress is a case where religious freedom and the rights of women are portrayed to be in conflict but in reality they are in sync.

In some Middle Eastern countries, women are forced to dress in a certain way because of religious tradition even if they don't support this tradition. Meanwhile, in Europe, secularists are telling women they cannot wear religious dress even if they want to as an expression of their faith.

Putting aside the fact that any man who tells women what clothes to wear needs his head examined, both cases are violations of both the religious freedom of women and their fundamental rights as women to make decisions in their own lives. In both cases, the state is acting paternalistically and restricting the religious freedom of women. In both cases, religious or secular elites are saying they know what is best for women. A respect for religious freedom would allow women to wear what they want in both situations. In other words, religious freedom empowers the woman to make her own decisions.

I am not saying that all conflict between religious freedom and women's rights can be easily resolved, but it is important to look for potential synergies between the two. This would be helpful to the advocates of both causes. They need not be seen as two essentially contradictory human rights norms.

Certainly proponents of women's rights and religious freedom can agree that forced conversion and marriages of abducted girls is wrong on both counts. Likewise, telling a woman that she cannot change her religion, that she cannot fall in love and choose her own husband, that she can be mutilated, that she cannot be educated or have political rights—all this is not only violating her rights as a woman, they are violating her rights to believe and act on her own beliefs.

Freedom of religion for women should be a strongly articulated goal of feminists who believe that women have the right to make their own decisions. The rights of women, who are most vulnerable to religious discrimination, should also be a strongly articulated goal of religious freedom advocates who believe that all people, especially vulnerable populations, should have the right of religious freedom.

Working together, advocates of religious freedom and women's rights could be a strong, bipartisan force that could make a difference is the lives of millions of women around the world. Disagreements over some issues should not lead to constant warfare. Rather, both sides need to focus on how they can work together on those issues about which they agree.

In France a Burqa Ban Protects Women

Cheryl Brumley

In the following viewpoint, Cheryl Brumley raises the question of if France's ban on the burqa protects or persecutes women. On one hand, she argues, it strips women of their religious freedom and beliefs. But on the other hand, there have been cases where the ban has actually protected women from being verbally and physically attacked. The author also quotes another woman who feels that the burqa serves as a sign of submission and states that she is in favor of the ban. Brumley is an independent radio reporter and producer based in London.

As you read, consider the following questions:

1. What is the Stasi Commission?
2. Why did Rayhana make international headlines in 2010?
3. Karimi says that rather than promoting harmony, the burqa ban specifically stigmatizes Muslim women and forces them to choose between what two things?

She points to a group of her characters, sketched out in pencil, taped to the wall. The movie she's working on is an adaptation of the play that brought her fame in France. It takes place in a bathhouse in Algeria. Most of the characters are dressed in robes and towels; one is dressed in a burqa.

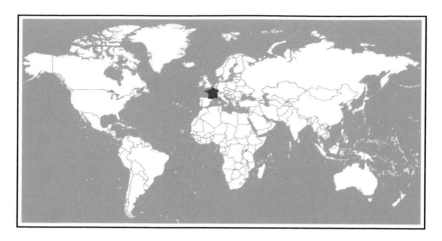

She says this character is "super Islamist," and not very nice. Her characterization isn't accidental. As a feminist in France, Rayhana has strong feelings about the burqa.

"You cannot be part of French society if you are wearing the burqa," she says. "The burqa is hiding the body and even the face."

Rayhana made international headlines in 2010 when she was attacked by two men on her way to the theater. They threw petrol on her and then tossed a cigarette at her face, which luckily didn't set her ablaze.

"It was something I didn't expect at all and it was really one of the most terrible days of my life," she says. "I still have nightmares about it."

She knew they were angry about her play, which was critical of Islam. Although she grew up Muslim, Rayhana, 51, is now an outspoken atheist. Although she thinks wearing the burqa is a choice, she says it is no less than a sign of women's inferiority. When the French Parliament banned it, she was all for it.

"For me the burqa is a sign of submission and what is submission? It means it negates liberty; it means that we're a slave. So I was really for this prohibition on the burqa," she says.

Philosopher Henri Pena Ruiz also supports the burqa ban.

"We cannot accept that someone is completely covered in France," he says. "It's a matter of which liberty we are choosing.

Austria's Ban on Full-Face Veils Comes into Force

Legislation banning full-face veils in public spaces went into effect in Austria on October 1.

The government says the law banning clothing such as the face-covering niqab or all-encompassing burqa is about protecting Austrian values and promotes integration.

Those who are stopped by police officers and refuse to take off their veils face a penalty of 150 euros ($176).

Muslim groups have condemned the ban, saying just a small minority of Muslims in Austria wear full-face veils.

The new rule is part of a package of policies that conservative Foreign and Integration Minister Sebastian Kurz initiated amid his drive to win the October 15 general elections.

France and Belgium introduced a ban on full-face veils in 2011. The European Court of Human Rights confirmed in July that such prohibitions are legal.

"Austria's Ban On Full-Face Veils Comes Into Force," Radio Free Europe/Radio Liberty,
October 1, 2017.

Are we choosing the right of a woman to show her face or are we choosing the right of a religious chief to impose the burqa?"

Henri was a member of the Stasi Commission, a group of 20 experts, lawyers, academics and former ministers who met in 2003 to review the place of laïcité—the French version of separation of church and state—in modern day France. The Stasi Commission met years before the so-called "burqa ban," at a time when France was preoccupied with religion's place in public grade schools.

"We didn't want to restrain personal expression. We wanted to say, 'You can express your religious views but not everywhere, and there are places where wearing these symbols can pose a problem,'" he says.

The commission ultimately recommended a ban on students and teachers wearing any kind of religious symbols in grade schools. This includes all Muslim headscarves, but also yarmulkes and crosses. According to Pena-Ruiz, their intent was to shield students from conflict.

"Though it may appear that we are limiting liberty, we are actually protecting the liberty of these young people," he says. "A school is a place of study and the school must focus on what is common to the students, not on their differences."

As another scholar put it, laïcité ensures that everybody in France is equal whether they like it or not. Supporters of laïcité say differences, like religion, only detract from shared values. But opponents say it unfairly targets France's Muslim population.

That means people like Hanane Karimi, who I meet in central Paris. She's wearing jeans, a red sweater, and a near-matching red hijab knotted tightly behind her head. As we walk on the street, she drops her head. She looks up and focuses her gaze only when talking to me or when reading the metro map. She's received some unwanted attention in the past.

"The first time I was with my little brother and an old woman with her grandchild says to me, 'What you are wearing is provocation.' I was really shocked," she says. "I could never imagine that someone could feel my veil is a provocation."

Karimi says that rather than promoting harmony, the burqa ban and the ban of religious symbols in grade schools specifically stigmatizes Muslim women and forces them to choose between their religion and their national identity.

She adds that one of the most damaging things about laïcité in France is that it conceals the real issues facing Muslim women. How do you fight chauvinism or racism — or any topic, really — if there isn't freedom of expression?

"I'm convinced if we don't put it in the public space, we don't have power to change," she says. "It is our right to speak about it. That is the challenge, to speak about what is taboo."

The French government shows no movement toward revisiting the ban on burqas. And right now, France is debating whether to extend the headscarf ban from grade schools to universities as well. Support is wide-reaching and includes former President Nicolas Sarkozy on the right and the current minister for women's rights on the left.

In Belgium a Ban on Face Veils Does Not Violate Human Rights

National Secular Society

In the following viewpoint, the National Secular Society reports on Belgium's ban on face veils in public spaces, which was upheld by the European Court of Human Rights, as it did not violate the European Convention on Human Rights. The ban was enacted to protect the rights and freedoms of others, but many women argue that the new law violates their rights. The court acknowledged it was a controversial decision but still ruled in favor of the ban. The National Secular Society campaigns for the separation of religion and state and equal respect for everyone's human rights.

As you read, consider the following questions:

1. What's the penalty for repeat offenders?
2. What year did Belgium ban the wearing of clothing, which obscures the wearer's identity in public places?
3. What was the first European country to issue a national ban on full-face veils in public?

The European Court of Human Rights has ruled that Belgium's ban on wearing face veils in public does not violate the European Convention on Human Rights.

The court ruled today that the restriction was justified because it was an attempt to protect "the rights and freedoms of others" which "sought to guarantee the conditions of living together." It

"European court backs Belgium's ban on face veils," National Secular Society, July 11, 2017. Reprinted by permission.

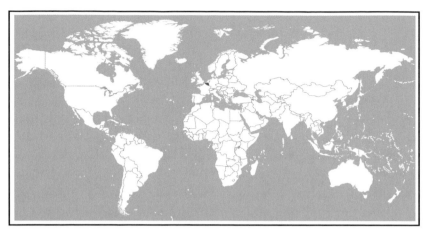

said the ban could be considered "proportionate" to those aims and "necessary in a democratic society."

In 2011 Belgium banned the wearing of clothing which obscures the wearer's identity in public places. This included partial or total face veils.

Two women who wanted to wear the niqab in public argued that the law had violated their rights under articles eight (right to respect for private and family life), nine (freedom of thought, conscience and religion) and 14 (prohibition of discrimination). The niqab, a burka most often worn by Muslim women, covers the whole body except the eyes.

Belgian national Samia Belcacemi said she had removed her veil in response to the law, fearing she might be fined or jailed. Moroccan national Yamina Oussar said she had chosen to stay at home, curtailing her social life.

The court said the ban was "controversial and undeniably carried risks in terms of the promotion of tolerance in society." But it ruled that no violation of the claimants' rights had taken place.

It said the law's drafting history showed that the authorities were attempting to promote public safety, gender equality and "a certain conception of living together." It said the state authorities were "better placed than an international court to assess the local needs and context."

And it said the punishment for breaking the law could be viewed as proportionate to the aims it was trying to promote. Those who defy the ban can be fined; repeat offenders can be imprisoned.

But the law is classified as a "hybrid" in Belgian law, meaning that municipal authorities can take alternative measures to uphold it.

The court also came to a similar judgement today over a bylaw banning face veils in the Belgian municipalities of Pepinster, Dison and Verviers.

In 2011 France became the first European country to issue a national ban on full-face veils in public. Since then Bulgaria and parts of the Netherlands, Switzerland, Germany, Spain and Italy have followed suit.

Earlier this year the German parliament supported a draft law banning women working in the civil service, judiciary and military from wearing full-face Islamic veils. Last month Norway's government proposed a burka ban in schools and universities. And the case comes as several French cities consider whether to introduce bans on the burkini, a full-body swimsuit, over the summer.

In 2014 the ECHR rejected arguments that the French ban on veils breached religious freedom and human rights. And in March the European Court of Justice ruled that workplace bans on the wearing of "any political, philosophical or religious sign," such as headscarves, did not necessarily constitute direct discrimination. But it added that such bans must be based on internal company rules requiring all employees to "dress neutrally."

The National Secular Society has serious concerns about the wearing of the burka and agrees that in some contexts it should be prohibited. However the NSS does not support legal attempts to ban it in all public places.

Stephen Evans, NSS campaigns director, said: "No woman should be forced to hide behind a burka. It is vital for civil society to expose the deeply intolerant view of women which the garment often symbolises. And freedom of religion is not absolute.

"But bans on clothing in public places are an unconvincing response to misogynistic attitudes.

"It should be stressed that the court's judgement is not a blank cheque to ban the burka across Europe. States that pass laws against face coverings are required to show that they have a legitimate aim in doing so and that they have handled the issue proportionately."

Restricting Religious Clothing Is an Attack on Tolerance and Pluralism

Kristin Lauria

In the following viewpoint, Kristin Lauria argues that banning or restricting religious apparel in secular nations erases the diverse global society the West was striving for in the past several decades. The author discusses how the terrorist attacks on 9/11 have led to more discrimination against Muslims and those who wear veils, thus changing the perception that we have of people who wear this type of religious clothing. Lauria is director of academic programs at the Euphrates Institute.

As you read, consider the following questions:

1. What location is also home to the continent's highest concentration of Muslims?
2. In how many western European countries have restrictions on Islamic covering been passed at the national or local level?
3. What is one of the reasons mentioned for the headscarf ban?

O ur five-part series on Veil Politics has examined how politics affect Muslim women's choice to cover, through mandating, promoting or forbidding the Islamic headscarf. In Iran women were forced to unveil before being required to don the chador under the

"No Veils Allowed?" by Kristin Lauria, Euphrates Institute, September 18, 2015. Reprinted by permission.

Islamic Republic. In Turkey, modernizing reforms sought to remove the veil from public life, preventing women's full participation in education and the workforce until recent shifts in policy led to droves of covered women entering the public domain. And in Afghanistan, the burqa came to symbolize all that was wrong with Taliban rule, but its politicization failed to change the fundamental experiences of women after the Taliban lost power.

In this final installment, we look at what happens when Muslim women's choice to wear the head scarf butts up against secular policies in the West, and we ask: is greater tolerance for differences the answer?

As we have seen, national policies across the Middle East have both restricted and required women's veiling. However, in the West, where individual rights are supposed to prevail, we might assume that individual choice – influenced, of course, by cultural and religious belonging and social identity – would determine whether Muslim women wear the veil.

Not necessarily so.

Muslim Veil Bans in the West

In at least eight western European countries restrictions on Islamic covering have been passed at the national or local levels. These include France, where a national ban (since 2004) prohibits the wearing of headscarves in schools and other public institutions and bans (since 2011) the niqab, (an Islamic head-covering which leaves only the eyes visible) in all public spaces; Belgium, which like France restricted veils that cover the face in 2011; and Italy, where a handful of towns have enacted restrictions on face-covering headscarves. In Germany, Spain and Denmark, local regulations also exist which prevent certain types of veiling in specific contexts.

In western Europe, prohibitions on the headscarf are most explicit and far-reaching in France, which is also home to the continent's highest concentration of Muslims, an estimated 5-6 million people. Whereas the 2004 ban applies more broadly to all religious symbols, including the yarmulkes and turbans worn by men in the Jewish and Sikh faiths, respectively, the 2011 restriction specifically targets the wearing of the niqab and the burqa in the public arena.

The reasons for the headscarf bans range from protection of women's rights to safeguarding "social cohesion," from ensuring national security to upholding state secularism (France's unique brand of secularism, termed laïcité, is enshrined in the French Constitution and dates back to the struggle between the State and the Catholic Church):

> The French government argues that the ban has wide public support. The authorities see the full-face veil not only as an affront to French secular values but also as a potential security risk, as it conceals a person's identity.

For a more nuanced exploration of the factors contributing to the ban, see *The Politics of the Veil* by Joan Wallach Scott.

The 2011 ban was upheld by the European Court of Human Rights on the basis that:

> the Court accepted that the barrier raised against others by a veil concealing the face in public could undermine the notion of "living together." In that connection, it indicated that it took into account the State's submission that the face played a significant role in social interaction. The Court was also able to understand the view that individuals might not wish to see,in places open to all, practices or attitudes which would fundamentally call into question the possibility of open interpersonal relationships, which, by virtue of an established consensus, formed an indispensable element of community life within the society in question.

Muslim and non-Muslim opponents, however, view the ban as hostile to individual rights:

> Critics accuse France of illiberalism, of curbing freedom of religious expression, and of imposing a Western interpretation of female oppression. Amnesty International, for example, called the recent European court ruling "a profound retreat for the right to freedom of expression and religion."

Diversity and Discrimination Post-9/11

Western veil bans bring to the fore an important question: how is peaceful coexistence achieved in a society comprised of diverse ethnic, cultural and religious groups?

Ideas such as multiculturalism, pluralism and tolerance for differences have come under fire in the post-9/11 world, as the rise of global terrorism has led to increasing incursions into citizens' private lives and limitations on what is considered acceptable in the public sphere.

The mulitculturalism that was a trademark policy of western European states in the late decades of the twentieth century has been called into question in recent years, with some worrying it has led to the increasing segregation of foreign communities from the rest of society, creating potential security risks or even breeding grounds for terrorism. In response, countries have increased citizenship requirements and shifted toward policies of integration or assimilation.

While currently there are no restrictions on the Islamic covering in the United States and the United Kingdom (in Canada, face covering is prohibited only during citizenship ceremonies), this does not mean that Muslim women in these countries do not face discrimination as a result of their religious attire. In one case heard by the U.S. Supreme Court, for instance, a young Muslim woman was denied employment at the clothing company Abercrombie & Fitch because her veil did not fit with the company's dress code.

In considering how we can best coexist despite (or perhaps because of!) our differences, I believe we must consider a further question: does a society become more harmonious as it becomes more homogenous (i.e. through the removal of religious and cultural symbols that distinguish us from one another), or is it possible that as we come to recognize our differences as an asset, rather than as a threat, tolerance and understanding will grow?

We conclude this series with some food for thought from scholar Lila Abu-Lughod:

Two points emerge from this fairly basic discussion of the meanings of veiling in the contemporary Muslim world, First, we need to work against the reductive interpretation of veiling as the quintessential sign of women's unfreedom, even if we object to state imposition of this form, as in Iran or with the Taliban, (It must be recalled that the modernizing states of Turkey and Iran had earlier in the century banned veiling and required men, except religious clerics, to adopt Western dress.) What does freedom mean if we accept the fundamental premise that humans are social beings, always raised in certain social and historical contexts and belonging to particular communities that shape their desires and understandings of the world? Is it not a gross violation of women's own understandings of what they are doing to simply denounce the burqa as a medieval imposition? Second, we must take care not to reduce the diverse situations and attitudes of millions of Muslim women to a single item of clothing, Perhaps it is time to give up the Western obsession with the veil and focus on some serious issues with which feminists and others should indeed be concerned.

Periodical and Internet Sources Bibliography

The following articles have been selected to supplement the diverse views presented in this chapter.

Qanta Ahmed, "As a Muslim, I strongly support the right to ban the veil," The Spectator, March 18, 2017, https://www.spectator.co.uk/2017/03/the-right-to-ban-the-veil-is-good-news-for-everybody-including-muslims/.

Ryan T. Anderson, "The Continuing Threat to Religious Liberty," National Review, August 3, 2017. https://www.nationalreview.com/2017/08/religious-liberty-under-attack/

Angelique Chrisafis, "France's headscarf war: 'It's an attack on freedom,'" July 22, 2013, https://www.theguardian.com/world/2013/jul/22/frances-headscarf-war-attack-on-freedom.

Lizzie Dearden, "Austrian parliament passes burqa ban seeing Muslim women face £130 fines for wearing full-face veils," May 18, 2017, http://www.independent.co.uk/news/world/europe/austria-burqa-ban-parliament-fines-150-full-face-veils-muslim-islam-niqabs-public-transport-a7742981.html.

Amanda Erickson, "France's Marine Le Pen refused to wear a headscarf to meet with Lebanese religious leaders," The Washington Post, February 23, 2017, https://www.washingtonpost.com/news/worldviews/wp/2017/02/23/marine-le-pen-refused-to-wear-a-headscarf-to-meet-with-lebanese-leaders/?utm_term=.d87e106cbd8a.

Nuno Ferreira, "German court rules against banning veil in schools, but Europe remains divided," The Conversation, March 23, 2015, https://theconversation.com/german-court-rules-against-banning-veil-in-schools-but-europe-remains-divided-39077.

Ashley Southall, "Religious Police Officers in New York Will Be Able to Wear Beards and Turbans," The New York Times, December 28, 2016. https://www.nytimes.com/2016/12/28/nyregion/new-york-police-department-sikh-beard-turban-policy.html

Isaac Weiner, "Accommodating Religion in the Workplace," OUP Blog, June 7, 2017. https://blog.oup.com/2017/06/religion-in-the-workplace/

For Further Discussion

Chapter 1
1. How did the burqa ban in France affect the country and its citizens?
2. Why is the headscarf seen as such a controversial article of religious clothing?

Chapter 2
1. What is the relationship between restricting religious clothing and women's rights?
2. What are two ways in which full-face veils have impacted women?

Chapter 3
1. How has the banning of certain religious articles of clothing affected students in public schools?
2. Why must US public school teachers be careful of how they teach and discuss religion with their students?

Chapter 4
1. How have the 9/11 terror attacks changed the perception of the veil?
2. Do you feel the banning of religious clothing is beneficial or harmful for a country? Why or why not?

Organizations to Contact

The editors have compiled the following list of organizations concerned with the issues debated in this book. The descriptions are derived from materials provided by the organizations. All have publications or information available for interested readers. The list was compiled on the date of publication of the present volume; the information provided here may change. Be aware that many organizations take several weeks or longer to respond to inquiries, so allow as much time as possible.

American Civil Liberties Union
125 Broad Street, 18th Floor, New York NY 10004
(212) 549-2500
website: www.aclu.org

The American Civil Liberties Union (ACLU) is an organization that has worked to defend the people's constitutional rights for nearly 100 years. Made up of more than 1.6 million members, the ACLU is also America's largest public interest law firm that fights to preserve freedom of religion. The ACLU is nonprofit and nonpartisan and is headquartered in New York City.

American Humanist Association
1821 Jefferson Place, NW, Washington, DC 20036
(202) 238-9088
email: aha@americanhumanist.org
website: https://americanhumanist.org/

The American Humanist Association has a sole goal to advance humanism and free belief in any god or supernatural force. For more than seventy years, the American Humanist Association has worked at creating a society where people can be good without a god, and where traditional religious faith is not required.

Americans for Religious Liberty

P.O.Box 6656, Silver Spring, MD 20916
(301) 460-1111
email: arlinc@verizon.net
website: www.arlinc.org

Americans for Religious Liberty is an organization that supports the separation of church and state. Founded in 1981, its mission statement reads that one of its missions is to "preserve the nation's historic traditions of religious, intellectual, and moral freedom in a secular state," according to its website.

Institutional Religious Freedom Alliance

312 Massachusetts Avenue, NE, Washington DC 20002
email: shapedbyfaith@irfalliance.org
website: www.irfalliance.org

The Institutional Religious Freedom Alliance is a faith-based organization that promotes religious freedom. The IRFA was founded by Dr. Stanley Carlson-Thies in 2008, who grew the organization out of an existing multi-faith network, called the Coalition to Preserve Religious Freedom. In September 2014, the IRFA became part of the Center for Public Justice.

Interfaith Alliance

2101 L St NW #400, Washington, DC 20037
(202) 466-0567
email: info@interfaithalliance.org
website: http://interfaithalliance.org

The Interfaith Alliance is an organization that celebrates religious freedom by promoting policies that protect religion and democracy. The organization believes that religious freedom is the foundation for democracy in America. The Interfaith Alliance was founded in 1994 and has members across the US from seventy-five different faith traditions.

People For the American Way
1101 15th St NW, Washington, DC 20005
(202) 467-4999
email: pfaw@pfaw.org
website: www.pfaw.org

People For the American Way is a nonprofit organization that works to further equal rights in America. Like many of the organizations already listed, this organization believes in religious freedom and equal justice for all Americans. The organization was founded in 1981 by Norman Lear, Barbara Jordan, and a group of business leaders.

Religious Freedom Coalition
PO Box 77511, Washington, DC 20013
(202) 543-0300
website: www.religiousfreedomcoalition.org

The Religious Freedom Coalition is a nonprofit organization that advocates for preservation of America's Christian heritage. The organization provides its services both nationally and internationally. The Religious Freedom Coalition was founded in 1982.

Religious Freedom Institute
1050 30th St NW, Washington, DC 20007
(202) 838-7734
email: rfi@religiousfreedominstitute.org
website: www.religiousfreedominstitute.org

The Religious Freedom Institute is an organization that has a plan to achieve acceptance of religious liberty around the world. The organization's plan to achieve its goal is based on convincing stakeholders in various regions that religious freedom would allow the stakeholders to achieve their own goals, whether they be political, economic, or religion.

Unitarian Universalist Association
24 Farnsworth St.
Boston, MA, 02210
(617) 742-2100
email: info@uua.org
website: www.uua.org/

The Unitarian Universalist Association is an organization made up of more than one thousand members. The organization is based on seven principles that include the worth of each person as well as the right to choose one's own beliefs. The organization is based on Christian faith and traditions.

United States Commission on International Religious Freedom
732 N. Capitol Street, N.W.
Suite A714
Washington, D.C. 20401
(202) 523-3240
email: media@uscirf.gov
website: www.uscirf.gov

The United States Commission on International Religious Freedom is an independent, bipartisan US federal government commission that is dedicated to fighting for religious freedom abroad. Being a government commission, the USCIRF are able to make recommendations and suggestions to people like the President, the Secretary of State, Congress, and more. The commission was created by the 1998 International Religious Freedom Act (IRFA).

Bibliography of Books

Melanie Adrian, *Religious Freedom at Risk: The EU, French Schools, and Why the Veil Was Banned.* New York, NY: Springer, 2016.

Waqar Ahmad and Ziauddin Sardar, *Muslims in Britain: Making Social and Political Space.* New York, NY: Routledge 2012.

John R. Bowen, *Why the French Don't Like Headscarves: Islam, the State, and Public Space.* Princeton, NJ: Princeton University Press, 2007.

Andrew Copson, *Secularism: Politics, Religion, and Freedom.* Oxford, UK: Oxford University Press, 2017.

Alessandro Ferrari and Sabrina Pastorelli, eds., *Burqa Affair Across Europe: Between Public and Private Space.* New York, NY: Routledge, 2018.

Silvio Ferrari and Sabrina Pastorelli, *Religion in Public Spaces: A European Perspective.* New York, NY: Routledge 2016.

David C. Gibbs, *Making Sense of Religion in America's Public Schools.* St. Petersburg, FL: The National Center for Life and Liberty, 2013.

Simone Hummert, *Religion in Public Schools.* Munich, Germany: GRIN Publishing, 2005.

Noel Merino, *Religion in Schools.* Detroit, MI: Greenhaven Publishing, 2012.

Michael D. Waggoner, *Religion in the Public Schools: Negotiating the New Commons.* Lanham, MD: Rowman & Littlefield Publishers, 2013.

Isaac Weiner, *Religion Out Loud: Religious Sound, Public Space, and American Pluralism.* New York, NY: New York University Press, 2014.

Linda K. Wertheimer, *Faith Ed: Teaching About Religion in an Age of Intolerance.* Boston, MA: Beacon Press, 2015.

Index

W

Z